石出和博

JAPANESE
BEAUTIFUL
RESIDENCE 2

KAZUHIRO ISHIDE

美しい 日本の 邸宅 2

忘れ去られてしまった
日本の美

ゆく河の流れは絶えずして、
しかももとの水にあらず
絶えず流れる河の急流に、
変わらぬ本質を見たのは鴨長明だが、
これを不易流行の理念へと高めたのは、
江戸時代の俳聖松尾芭蕉だった。

日本人は古来より四季の移ろい、
花鳥風月にあはれを覚え、
時の流れのなかに侘び寂びを見いだした。
神が宿るとされた森から切り出された木は
人間たちが住む家へ姿を変え、
何百年、何千年とこの国をつくってきた。

悠久の歴史のなかで変わるものは変わり、
変わらないものは変わらずに残る。
これを俳諧の世界では不易流行という。
例えば森は、何十年と変わらずに
そこに存在し続けているように見えるが、
実際はいくつもの小さな生と死の往還のなかで

絶えず変化を続け、その美しさを保っている。

伝統や文化も同じだ。

いつまでも変わらないもののなかに変わりゆくものがあり、

時代とともに受け継がれていく。

しかし戦後、経済成長と効率ばかりが優先された結果、

日本人の美や価値観は、いつのまにか

途絶えてしまったように思う。

街には看板が溢れかえり、

規格化された家々が所狭しと建ち並ぶ。

21世紀は、高齢社会となり、経済成長にも陰りが見え、

社会には相変わらず不安が絶えない。

今、私たちに求められているのは

便利さや効率だけではなく、

美しいものを築き、愛で、残していくことではあるまいか。

人は美しいもののなかで生きることで、

その生をいっそう輝かせることができる。

何も昔に戻ろうという話ではない。

日本人が築いてきたこの国に、家づくりを通して、

これまでに大切にしてきた美を取り戻していきたいのだ。

　　　石出和博

The Utterly Forgotten Beauty of Japan

Rivers flow on and on, unceasingly,
yet their waters are never the same.
In the constant flowing of rivers,
Kamo no Chomei saw an unchanging essence.
But it was Edo-period haiku master Matsuo Basho
who elevated this to the principle
of fueki-ryuko, immutability and fluidity.

Since ancient times, the Japanese have been
highly sensitive to the changing of seasons
and the beauties of nature.
In the passage of time, they see wabi-sabi,
beauty in simplicity and organic imperfection.
For thousands of years, they cut trees,
from the forests in which their gods dwelt,
refashioning them into human abodes,
making this country what it is.

In this long history, things subject to change have changed,
as immutable things have persisted.
In the world of haikai, this is known as fueki-ryuko.
Consider a forest, which for decades exudes an unvarying presence.
In reality, it is a melting pot of life and death in myriad forms,
a place of unremitting mutation, yet unwavering beauty.
The same applies to tradition and culture.
Amid things that never change are ever-changing things,
passed down to us through the ages.

In post-war Japan, however, as economic growth and efficiency
became the predominant concerns, the aesthetics and values
of the Japanese seem to have dried up, almost unnoticed.
Everywhere, cramped, newly built cookie-cutter houses
appeared on streets overflowing with signboards.

In the 21st century, this aging society, beset by economic gloom,
remains as anxious as ever.
Rather than economic growth, convenience, or efficiency,
we need to build, love, and conserve beautiful things.
It is by living amidst beautiful things
that we can make our lives shine more brightly.

This doesn't mean returning to the past,
but rather trying to recapture that beauty
that Japanese have always held to be important,
as expressed in the houses and culture they produced for so long.

Kazuhiro Ishide

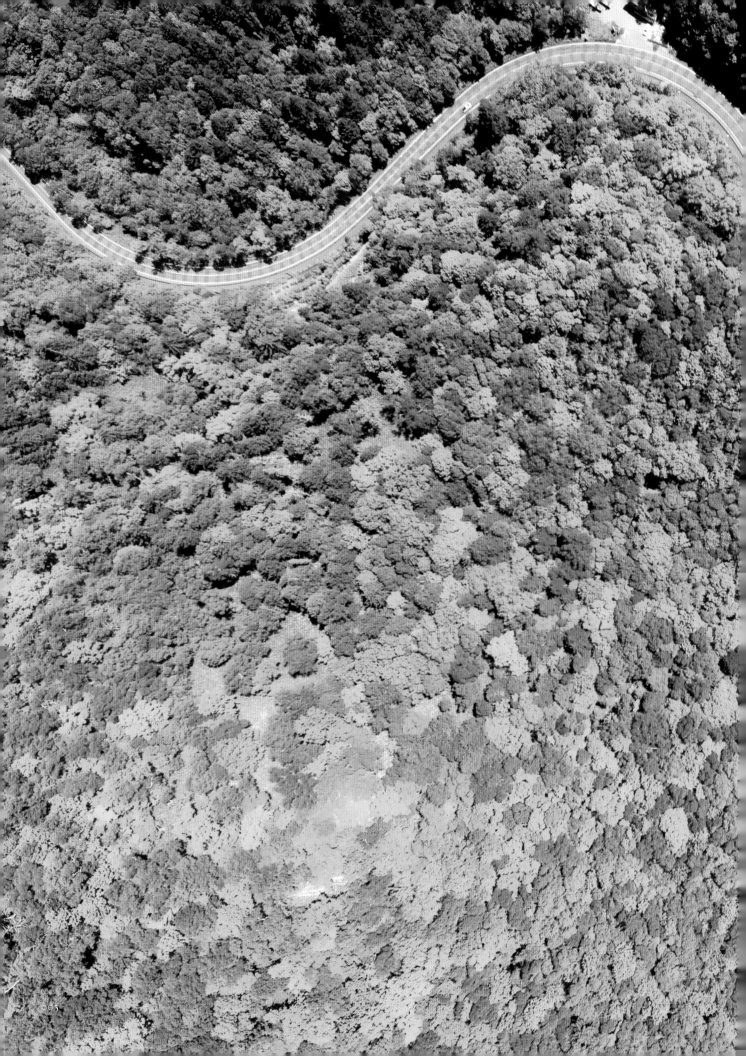

Contents

Japanese Beautiful Residence 2

1

Chapter 1 : Residences that Lend Color to Life

第 1 章　暮らしに彩りを添える邸宅

木材の質感に触れる家
A Residence for Feeling the Texture of Wood

ホールは優美な曲線を描く階段が2階まで伸びやかに続く。

木材の質感に触れる家
A Residence for Feeling the Texture of Wood

ホールの両側の開口を幾何学のステンドグラスが彩る。

生命が呼応する空間

森や大地が育んだ天然の木や石には生命力が宿る。
それらの素材を一つひとつ吟味し、空間へと活かす。
自然の素材がもつ深遠な美を感じさせる邸宅が、ここに誕生した。

Spaces that Engage with Life

Natural wood and stone nurtured by forest and earth have a life force.
The way each material is employed in this space is deeply considered.
Here is a residence that evokes the profound beauty of natural materials.

木材の質感に触れる家
A Residence for Feeling the Texture of Wood

木材の質感に触れる家
A Residence for Feeling the Texture of Wood

1.光を透過したステンドグラスが外観に華やかさを添えている。
2.玄関床は御影石の組み込みデザインとした。

木材の質感に触れる家
A RESIDENCE FOR FEELING THE TEXTURE OF WOOD

グレーの花崗岩と深い軒によって構成された端正な外観。

Profoundly Beautiful Materials

An imposing granite exterior, with deep eaves that cast beautiful shadows. This residence makes striking use of wood and stone, and various other materials, all of which tell their own stories. To source the right granite for the exterior walls, the owner made a special trip to a quarry near the Swiss-Italian border.

The walls and floors of the more public areas, such as the living room and hall, feature beige marble to soft effect. All the stone was purchased in raw form from Italy and China to be processed specifically for the residence. This made it possible to realize the huge marble facing boards, 3 m wide, 90 cm deep, and 15 cm high, to accentuate the raised sections of the entryway and the Japanese-style room.

If stone were used for everything, the space would appear too harsh, but solid wood such as tamo (Japanese ash) and hiba (hinoki cypress) add softness. The living room, which connects to the garden, has a lattice ceiling of tamo, while the entry hall, with its gracefully curved staircase, features a ceiling of hiba that harmonizes with the geometric patterns of the stained-glass windows.

The wood used in the private spaces was obtained by selecting only the finest quality grain patterns from various logs of sawn tamo and nara (oak). For the pillars of the Japanese-style rooms, special straight-grain knot-free sugi cedar was procured on a dedicated trip to Yoshino in Nara Prefecture. The boards used for the ceiling and floor are made from 1,000-year-old sugi trees from Ichifusa (Kumamoto Prefecture), while the lacquered floor boards in the tokonoma alcove were finished by artisans in Wajima (Ishikawa Prefecture).

The life force and stories of these solid materials give rise to a peerless residence of profound beauty.

木材の質感に触れる家
A Residence for Feeling the Texture of Wood

木の格子天井が空間に陰影と立体感をもたらす。

木材の質感に触れる家
A RESIDENCE FOR FEELING THE TEXTURE OF WOOD

庭に面して上下階にリビングを配置している。

3 2 1

1.2階のリビングは切妻天井を活かして照明をデザインしている。
2.1階にはプライベートジムも用意した。
3.バスルームには御影石を用いた。

ステンレスワイヤーのなめらかな手すりは連続するよう製作した。

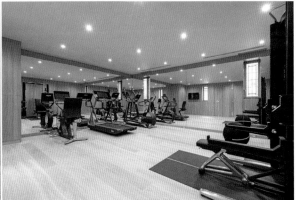

波打つような欄間のデザインがモダンな印象を与えている。床柱には市房杉を使用。

木材の質感に触れる家
A Residence for Feeling the Texture of Wood

1
―
2

1.和室の設計は和庭との連続性を重視した。
2.組子欄間が和室を緩やかに区切っている。

材料の深遠な美

　花崗岩を用いた重厚感のある外観に、深い軒が美しい陰影を描く――。この邸宅には木や石などいくつもの材料が使われているが、それらすべてに物語がある。オーナーは外壁の花崗岩を選ぶため、イタリアとスイスの国境近くにある石切場まで足を運び、原石を確認したほどだ。

　リビングやホールなどのパブリックスペースは、床・壁ともに柔らかい印象のベージュの大理石を使用。石はすべてイタリアと中国から原石で購入し、この邸宅に合わせて加工した。このような手順を踏んだからこそ、玄関や和室に用いた幅３ｍ、奥行き90㎝、高さ15㎝という巨大な大理石の框を実現することができたのだ。

　すべてに石を使うと空間が硬い印象になってしまうが、そこに柔らかさを添えているのがタモやヒバなどの無垢の木である。庭とつながるリビングはタモの格子天井に。優美な曲線を描く階段のあるホールは天井にヒバを用い、幾何学模様のステンドグラスと調和させている。

　プライベートスペースではタモ、ナラの丸太を何本も製材し、良質な木目のみを使用。和室の柱などは奈良県の吉野方向き、無節の特別な柾目の杉まで出向き、無節の特別な柾目の杉を入手した。天井板と床板は、樹齢1000年の市房杉からつくり、床の間の漆塗りの地板は輪島の職人が仕上げた。

　無垢の素材たちがもつ生命力と物語により、深遠な美を宿す唯一無二の邸宅が生まれた。

暮らしの音が聞こえる家
A RESIDENCE AWAKE TO THE SOUNDS OF LIFE

中庭に面した寝室横のテラスにはジェットバスを備える。

暮らしの音が聞こえる家
A RESIDENCE AWAKE TO THE SOUNDS OF LIFE

028

空間がつくるグルーヴ

家族と暮らす日常も、ゲストを招く賑やかなパーティーのときも、上質な音楽とゆったりと流れる時間がそこにはある。屋外と連続する開放的な空間が、心地よい音を響かせる。

Grooves Carved Out of Space

Whether an ordinary day with family, or partying merrily with guests,
this place is designed for leisurely listening to exquisite music.
The open space connected with the outdoors resounds with pleasant music.

暮らしの音が聞こえる家
A RESIDENCE AWAKE TO THE SOUNDS OF LIFE

1. 中庭にアウトドア家具を置き、室内の延長で使える場所にした。
2. 壁のスリットから風が抜けるよう設計。

暮らしの音が聞こえる家
A Residence Awake to the Sounds of Life

中庭の吹き抜けを介して上下階の様子が伝わる。

暮らしの音が聞こえる家
A Residence Awake to the Sounds of Life

1.艶やかな床のタイルが光を反射し、室内が明るくなる。
2.光庭にはオリーブのシンボルツリーを植えた。
3.華やかな印象のダイニング。

2

1

3

暮らしの音が聞こえる家
A RESIDENCE AWAKE TO THE SOUNDS OF LIFE

オーディオ機器のためリビングの一角を舞台のようにしつらえた。

暮らしの音が聞こえる家
A RESIDENCE AWAKE TO THE SOUNDS OF LIFE

石とフロストガラスによるスタイリッシュな外観。

Quality Hobby Time

A busy road runs in front of this residence, surrounded by high-density housing in an inner-city area. The owner wished to live in open space without worrying about privacy. He wanted to uninhibitedly enjoy his hobbies with guests. Our proposal was to create a courtyard and a light court as spaces that are open to the inside of the home but closed to the outside world.

The exterior has a simple box-like appearance. Above the garage at ground level, a two-story living space cloaked in an external wall of chopped limestone. The frosted glass sheets inlaid on the road side diffuse light, guiding soft light through the courtyard into the interior. The open living-dining-kitchen (LDK) area with 3-meter ceilings

can also serve as a reception space for large parties. Beige tiles are used on the floor, chopped limestone on the wall. The adjoining courtyard and light garden are also rendered in the same materials, creating a spatial continuity between inside and outside and a distinct sense of openness. In one corner of the living room, a massive pair of audio speakers is installed.

On the floor above the LDK is a spacious bedroom of 45 m². A jacuzzi bath and outdoor shower on the extended terrace create a resort hotel-like atmosphere.

The basement is a space dedicated to hobbies. At the entrance is a space for exhibiting the owner's collection for the delight of guests. Even the garage is equipped with a high-end audio system. This residence is certainly ideal for indulging in relaxation and entertainment.

1.ガラス越しにホールからガレージの内部が見える。
2.ホールの一角にはバイクを展示するスペースを設けた。

暮らしの音が聞こえる家
A Residence Awake to the Sounds of Life

1
___
2

1.周囲の視線を気にすることなく、ジェットバスを楽しめる。
2.フロストガラスによって柔らかな光となる。

上質な趣味の時間

前面道路は交通量が多く、周囲は住宅が密集する都心部という立地。オーナーは周囲からの目線を気にすることなく、開放的な暮らしを希望した。さらに、ゲストともに心おきなく楽しい趣味の時間を過ごしたい。そこで提案したのが、中庭と光庭を設け、外に閉じ内に開く空間構成だった。

外観は箱のようなシンプルなたたずまい。ガレージが入る1階の上に、石を割ったままのような自然な風合いを残す割肌のライムストーンの壁に覆われた2層の居住スペースが展開される。道路側に嵌め込んだフロストガラスが光を拡散し、中庭を通じて柔らかな光が室内へと導く。

天井高3mのLDKは多人数でのパーティーに対応するレセプションスペースでもある。床と壁はベージュのタイル、壁は割肌のライムストーン。隣接する中庭と光庭も同じ素材で仕上げて連続させ、室内に広がりと開放感が生まれた。リビングの一角にはこだわりのオーディオスピーカーを設置している。

LDKの上階は25畳を超える寝室。連続するテラスにはジェットバス、アウトドアシャワーを設け、リゾートホテルのような雰囲気を演出した。

一方の地下は趣味を楽しむ空間。エントランスには収蔵品の展示スペースを設け、ゲストの目を楽しませる。ガレージにもオーディオを備えており、まさに趣味を堪能できる住まいである。

日々の瞬間を彩る家
A Residence that Colors the Moments of the Day

日常という名の物語

真の豊かさとは、何気ない日常のなかに喜びがあること。
穏やかな和のしつらえと趣味を享受する部屋、内に開く開放的な空間が、
日常に彩りをもたらし、何世代にも引き継がれる邸宅となる。

Stories of Everyday Life

True wealth is to find joy in the ordinary moments of daily life.
Calming Japanese decorative elements, rooms for pursuing hobbies, and spaces open to the interior add color to daily life;
a residence fit to be passed on for generations to come.

中庭には広々としたデッキテラスを設け、室内のように家具を配置した。

日々の瞬間を彩る家
A RESIDENCE THAT COLORS THE MOMENTS OF THE DAY

格子や組子、網代など和のモチーフを随所に取り入れた。

日々の瞬間を彩る家
A RESIDENCE THAT COLORS THE MOMENTS OF THE DAY

1
―
2

1.中庭を1段掘り下げることで緑を近くに感じられる。
2.障子越しの光や間接照明が陰影を感じさせる雰囲気をつくり出す。

ダイニングは緑と光を感じながら食事を楽しめる。

日々の瞬間を彩る家
A RESIDENCE THAT COLORS THE MOMENTS OF THE DAY

コンクリート打ちっ放しの壁が外界からの視線を遮る。

052

玄関ホールの横に茶室を配置し、茶会もできるようにした。

Richness that Opens up from Within

The exterior along the road, of concrete walls and virtually no windows, evokes a museum. Yet, beyond the tunnel-like approach, one enters a surprisingly bright and open courtyard.

The owner wanted versatile spaces that would allow for two or three generations to live together in the future. Exploiting the site's gently sloping topography, about half of the ground floor was buried underground to enable a ceiling height of 6 meters. The courtyard was also boldly excavated. Most of the rooms are positioned to look onto the courtyard. A glass screen was erected on top of the concrete wall on the street side, both to let light into the courtyard and to soften the visual impact on the streetscape. Closing the courtyard to the outside and opening it to the inside offers private open-space living without the need for curtains, despite the high-density residential location.

The interior of the house is decorated with colors, materials, and motifs associated with traditional Japanese-style furnishing and decorative elements. Extensive use is made of classic Japanese materials such as diatomaceous earth (for painting the walls), kumiko-style shoji screens (with traditional Japanese muntins), washi paper, tamo (Japanese ash), and sugi cedar to heighten the appeal of the interior materials. At the same time, the three-dimensional spatial composition and generous volume give the rooms a modern feel.

The couple owning the house also paid close attention to spaces for entertainment, including a theater room to fulfill a dream of the husband's. For the wife, who is fond of the tea ceremony, the residence includes a formal Japanese-style room, complete with a cupboard for tea-ceremony vessels and implements, a machiai waiting bench, and a large dairo sunken hearth for preparing tea.

In this residence, all the family members can live comfortably for many years, happily pursuing and enjoying their respective hobbies .

1.8畳の和室には障子越しに明るい光が入る。
2.茶庭と中庭の間に塀を立て、世界観をつくり出した。

日々の瞬間を彩る家
A Residence that Colors the Moments of the Day

スポットライトが愛車を照らすショールームのようなガレージ。

日々の瞬間を彩る家
A RESIDENCE THAT COLORS THE MOMENTS OF THE DAY

1
―――
2

1.中庭に面したトレーニングルーム。
2.シアタールームは最新のプロ用音響機器を導入し、専門家にチューニングを依頼した。

カーテンが必要ない開放的な空間を実現している。

日々の瞬間を彩る家
A Residence that Colors the Moments of the Day

1
2

1.吹き抜けのダイニングに対し、リビングは天井を低く抑え落ちついた雰囲気に。
2.2階は吹き抜け越しにスタディースペースがある。

内に開く豊かさ

道路沿いにコンクリート壁を建てた外観にはほとんど窓がなく、美術館を彷彿とさせる。トンネルのようなアプローチを抜けると、驚くほど明るく開放的な中庭が広がっている。

オーナーは将来的に2世代、3世代で同居することを見据えた可変性のある空間を求めた。敷地の緩やかに傾斜する地形を活かし、1階を半分ほど地中に埋めることで6mという天井高を確保し、中庭も大胆に掘り下げた。主な居室は中庭に面するように配置。道路側のコンクリート壁の上部をガラススクリーンとし、中庭に光を取り入れると同時に、街並みに圧迫感を与えないよう配慮した。外に閉じ内側に開くことで、住宅街にありながら開放的な空間とカーテンの必要ない暮らしを叶えている。

室内は、和のしつらえをテーマとした色や素材、モチーフを採用。珪藻土による塗り壁、組子障子、和紙、タモや杉材など和の素材を多用し、素材の魅力を際立たせつつも、立体的な空間構成やボリューム感によってモダンにまとめ上げている。

オーナー夫妻の趣味の空間にもこだわり、ご主人の夢でもあった本格的なシアタールームを実現した。また、お茶を嗜む奥さまのために、水屋や待合も備え、大炉のお点前もできる正統派の和室をしつらえた。家族全員が趣味やこだわりを楽しみながら、長きにわたって住み続けられる邸宅が完成した。

Chapter 2 : Residences that Look Out on the Four Seasons of Japan

第 2 章　日本の四季折々の景観を望む邸宅

季節の訪れを知らせる家

A RESIDENCE THAT INTIMATES THE ARRIVAL OF THE SEASONS

変わりゆく景色

この邸宅では、時を刻むものは時計ではない。
刻一刻と移り変わる窓外の景色と、光と影が時の流れを紡いでいく。
ともに景色を眺めながら、温かな空間で家族は思い思いに過ごす。

Everchanging Landscapes

In this residence, time is not marked by the clock.
Outside the windows, the scenery changes moment to moment, light and shadow spinning the flow of time.
As they take in the scenery from the warm interior, the family passes the time together, each in their own way.

ペンダントライトが空間のスケールを強調する。

季節の訪れを知らせる家
A RESIDENCE THAT INTIMATES THE ARRIVAL OF THE SEASONS

コーナーリビングは2面をガラス窓が囲っている。

季節の訪れを知らせる家
A Residence that Intimates the Arrival of the Seasons

2階へと続く階段ホールは照明器具を用いたアクセントのあるデザイン。

季節の訪れを知らせる家
A RESIDENCE THAT INTIMATES THE ARRIVAL OF THE SEASONS

Experiencing the Changing Scenery

The enormous living room boasts a 6-meter-high ceiling. As if viewing a panoramic video, through the huge 6-meter-high rectangular panes of the glass curtain, the house occupants enjoy a snowy landscape; the snow glistens in the sunlight of the day, and twinkles under a starry sky in the darkness of night.

The use of such massive areas of glass makes heating and cooling a challenge. The residence thus features a geothermal heat pump to control the heating and cooling of the entire building. Along with the brightness of the sun, the windows let in warmth, with underfloor heating efficiently delivering the rest of the necessary heat.

A built-in fireplace in the dividing wall with the adjoining reception room, finished in dark gray tiles, asserts a strong presence. It was designed so that flickering flames of fire can be seen from both spaces. This heat of the fireplace also helps to warm the living room.

The kitchen and other sink and basin areas were designed to be pleasant and comfortable, as well as easy to use. Behind the kitchen there is a pantry and housekeeping area with ample storage space, and beside the shower room is a utility room. There is also a laundry chute in the dressing room of the second-floor bathroom to help achieve a compact and efficient housekeeping workflow. The terrace that adjoins the dining room offers a view of the outside world with an atmosphere quite different from that of the living room.

Sip on a drink at the corner bar in the living room, or immerse yourself in a hobby in your room. This house offers a warm, comfortable indoor space for families, each member spending time as they please, all the while enjoying nature to their heart's content.

1.リビングとダイニングに囲まれた場所にテラスを配置した。
2.玄関正面にはディスプレイスペースを設けた。

1

2

季節の訪れを知らせる家
A Residence that Intimates the Arrival of the Seasons

温かな照明の室内が雪景色に浮かび上がる。

暖炉と薪置き場は空間に合わせて造作した。

移ろいを感じる

リビングは天井高6mもの大空間。6m四方の大きなガラスカーテンウォールからは、昼は陽光に輝く雪景色を、夜は闇に煌めく星空を楽しめる。

これだけ大きなガラス窓を設けると、冷暖房が課題となる。この邸宅では地熱ヒートポンプを導入し、全館で冷暖房を一括コントロールする設計とした。ガラス窓から太陽の明るさと同時に暖かさをも取り入れ、床暖房も設置することで、温熱問題を見事にクリアした。

隣接する応接室の仕切り壁二面を存在感のあるダークグレーのタイルで仕上げ、暖炉を造作。どちらの空間からもゆらめく炎を眺められるデザインにした。その暖気がリビングも暖めてくれる。

キッチンなどの水まわりは、心地よさと同時に快適さや使い勝手を追求した。キッチンの裏には十分な収納量の食品庫と家事コーナーを、シャワールームの横にはユーティリティーを用意。2階バスルームの脱衣室にはランドリーシューターを設置し、コンパクトかつ効率的な家事動線を実現した。

ダイニングにはテラスが隣接し、リビングとは違った雰囲気で外の眺めを楽しめる。

リビングの一角のバーコーナーでグラスを傾けたり、自室で趣味に没頭したりなど、暖かく快適な屋内で自然を存分に味わいながら、家族が思い思いの時間を過ごせる邸宅である。

大窓で景色を堪能する家

A RESIDENCE WITH HUGE WINDOWS FOR SAVORING THE SCENERY

自然の懐の深さ

時の流れは本質を問う。美しいものは時を経るほどに深みを増し、
本物は古びることなく、熟していく。
家族が積み重ねる時間と自然の移ろいが、空間の彩りとなる。

外観には石や金属など多様な素材を用いた。

The Depth of Nature's Heart

In time, the essence of things becomes known. In time, true beauty grows deeper and genuine things age and mature; they do not grow old.
The accumulated time spent together by families and the changes of nature color the spaces.

大窓で景色を堪能する家
A Residence with Huge Windows for Savoring the Scenery

景色を堪能できる大窓から自然光を取り入れる。

大窓で景色を堪能する家
A RESIDENCE WITH HUGE WINDOWS FOR SAVORING THE SCENERY

1.湾曲したガラスの大窓に空の景色が映り込む。
2.テラスの一部は屋根を設けず、抜けをつくった。

大窓で景色を堪能する家
"A Residence with Huge Windows for Savoring the Scenery

Two Streams of Time

This residence was conceived with two streams of time in mind; the flow of a day and a long flow of 10 or 20 years.

Overlooking the sea to its south and grand mountains to its west, the large atrium-style living room space features massive windows that extend for two floors to the ceiling. The curved line of these windows enables a panoramic view out on the magnificent scenery.

The shadows of window frames and beams shift sundial-like throughout the day as the sun crosses the sky. At night, light seeps gently out, giving the room the look of a beautiful lantern seen from afar. The scenery visible through the windows changes with the seasons, signaling their shifts from one to another.

The long passage of time can be unexpectedly brutal, because it washes away that which is superficial to reveal the true nature of things. This residence is a "genuine home" that will grow in charm with the years of family life accumulated within it. Materials such as solid nara oak, tamo ash columns, and natural quartz were selected precisely for their tendency to become more appealing with use. Their colors and textures were used to give the space its refined character.

The history of accumulated time spent in the house by the family adds to the atmosphere and expression of the spaces. A residence is a container for living, and a "genuine home" allows for all kinds of lifestyles. One can look forward to seeing how the charm of such a residence grows over 10 or 20 years.

彫刻のような階段が出迎える。

大窓で景色を堪能する家
A RESIDENCE WITH HUGE WINDOWS FOR SAVORING THE SCENERY

照明によって優美な曲線が強調される。

アイアンの手すりが緩やかなスパイラルを描く。

大窓で景色を堪能する家
A RESIDENCE WITH HUGE WINDOWS FOR SAVORING THE SCENERY

$$\frac{1}{3 \quad 2}$$

1.光と影が刻一刻と移ろい、時の流れを感じさせる。
2.洗面室は水をテーマに水槽を配した。
3.落ちついた雰囲気のバスルーム。

2つの時の流れ

この邸宅には、2つの時の流れがある。1つは1日の流れ、もう1つは10年、20年という長い時間の流れである。

南側は海、西側には雄大な山々を望む立地であることから、リビングは2層吹き抜けの大空間とし、天井高まである大窓を設けた。大窓を湾曲させることでパノラマスクリーンのように壮大な景色を一望できる。

太陽が移動するにつれ、窓枠や梁の影も移動し、陰影が日時計のように変化していく。夜は室内からの明かりがふわりと外にもれ、遠くから眺めるとまるで美しいランタンのようだ。窓外の景色は四季折々

に変化し、季節の移ろいを告げてくれる。

長い時の流れは、思いのほか残酷である。なぜなら、本質をさらけ出すからだ。この邸宅は、家族の時間が積み重ねられることで味わいを増す"本物の家"をつくりたいという思いが込められている。ナラ無垢材、タモの柱、天然のクォーツなど、使うほどに魅力が深まる素材を選び、それぞれの色や質感を活かして空間へと昇華させた。

空間に趣や表情を添えるのが、そこで暮らす家族の時間と積み重ねられる歴史である。家とは暮らしを受けとめる器であり、"本物の家"はあらゆる暮らしを許容する。10年後、20年後の変化が楽しみになる、そんな邸宅に仕上がった。

風景に溶け込む家
A RESIDENCE THAT MERGES INTO THE LANDSCAPE

2面のガラス窓から光が入り、明るい印象のLDK。

風景に溶け込む家
A RESIDENCE THAT MERGES INTO THE LANDSCAPE

抽象的な具体性

雄大な景色を背景に、多様なテイストが共存する邸宅。
立体的に変化する空間構成が、あらゆるものを許容する。
それぞれの魅力が響き合い、一つの大きな個性が生まれた。

Abstract Concreteness

A residence that accommodates diverse tastes, against a backdrop of magnificent scenery.
A spatial composition that changes in three dimensions allows all kinds of possibilities.
The charms of its different aspects resonate to create a highly individual whole greater than the sum of its parts.

風景に溶け込む家
A RESIDENCE THAT MERGES INTO THE LANDSCAPE

水平ラインを強調したシャープな外観。

風景に溶け込む家
A Residence that Merges into the Landscape

1.大窓から雄大な景色を望む。
2.2つのペンダントライトが天井高を強調する。
3.キッチンは照明でクールに演出。

風景に溶け込む家
A Residence that Merges into the Landscape

ガレージの一角にはバイクの駐輪スペースを設けた。

風景に溶け込む家
A RESIDENCE THAT MERGES INTO THE LANDSCAPE

グレーやブラウンを基調にしたシックな書斎。

風景に溶け込む家
A Residence that Merges into the Landscape

Tolerance for Diversity

How can diverse tastes be harmoniously combined in a single space? This residence offers a brilliant answer to this conundrum.

To leverage the sloping site, a split-level layout was used, moving up a half-floor at a time. The entrance way on the ground floor (Level 1) is a simple space with a unified chic, monotone look, illuminated by abstract light diffusing through frosted glass. A half-floor higher, on the second level, is a living-dining-kitchen (LDK) space, while a half-floor down is a Japanese-style room and study.

The LDK space on Level 2 is designed to allow circulation around a courtyard. The stylish interior features dark brown flooring offset by the white sofa and kitchen. Framed with dark brown panels, the kitchen visually evokes a theater stage.

With its gray tones, the design of the study is elegantly subdued, whereas in the powder room, glossy white coloring creates a more sumptuous look. Like this, each space has its own atmosphere to savor, in line with its purpose.

Remarkably, the different tastes, of simplicity, elegance, and stylishness, come together in a single residence without discordance, thanks to the split-level architectural composition. The distance from room to room, and the way sight lines change slowly due to the gradual shift in elevation across the split levels, seem to organically connect the different moods of the spaces.

This is a residence that takes skillful advantage of site topography and accommodates exceptional stylistic diversity.

1.和室はゲストルームも兼ねている。
2.玄関ホールから半階上にキッチンが垣間見える。

1

2

風景に溶け込む家
A Residence that Merges into the Landscape

角に扉を設けた玄関。ミラーが広がりをもたらす。

多様性の許容

　多様なテイストを一つの空間に収めるには、どのような方法があるだろうか——。

　この邸宅は、その難問に見事な解答を導き出した。

　傾斜地という立地を活かし、半階ずつ上がるスキップフロアの空間構成を採用。1階の玄関はモノトーンでシックに統一し、フロストガラス越しの抽象的な光が広がるシンプルな空間とした。半階上がると2階のLDKへ、半階下がると和室や書斎へとつながる。

　2階のLDKは中庭を中心に回遊できる。ダークブラウンの床材に白のソファやキッチンカウンターが映えるスタイリッシュな

インテリア。キッチンはダークブラウンのパネルでフレーミングし、舞台のようでもある。

　一方の書斎はグレーを基調にシックにまとめた。さらにパウダールームは艶めく白がゴージャスな雰囲気を醸すなど、それぞれの空間の用途に合わせて、異なるテイストを楽しむことができる。

　シンプルやエレガント、スタイリッシュと異なるテイストも、スキップフロアだからこそ、それぞれの魅力がぶつかることなく、一つの邸宅としてまとめ上げられている。部屋から部屋への距離を取り、スキップフロアによる緩やかな高低差で視線が徐々に変わるため、それぞれのテイストが自然につながっている。

　地形を巧みに利用した、多様性を許容する邸宅である。

天然素材を活かした家
A RESIDENCE THAT MAKES USE OF NATURAL MATERIALS

深い軒のおかげでバルコニーでも快適に過ごせる。

暮らしの本質

日常を輝かせるのは、心ゆくまで楽しめる非日常。
エンターテインメント性とくつろぎを追求し、
北海道の大自然と一つになれるコンドミニアムが誕生した。

The Essence of Living

It is the little extraordinary things of life that gladden the heart and light up everyday life.
This ski lodge-residence, designed with entertainment and relaxation in mind,
makes the occupants feel at one with the mighty nature of Hokkaido.

天然素材を活かした家
A RESIDENCE THAT MAKES USE OF NATURAL MATERIALS

102

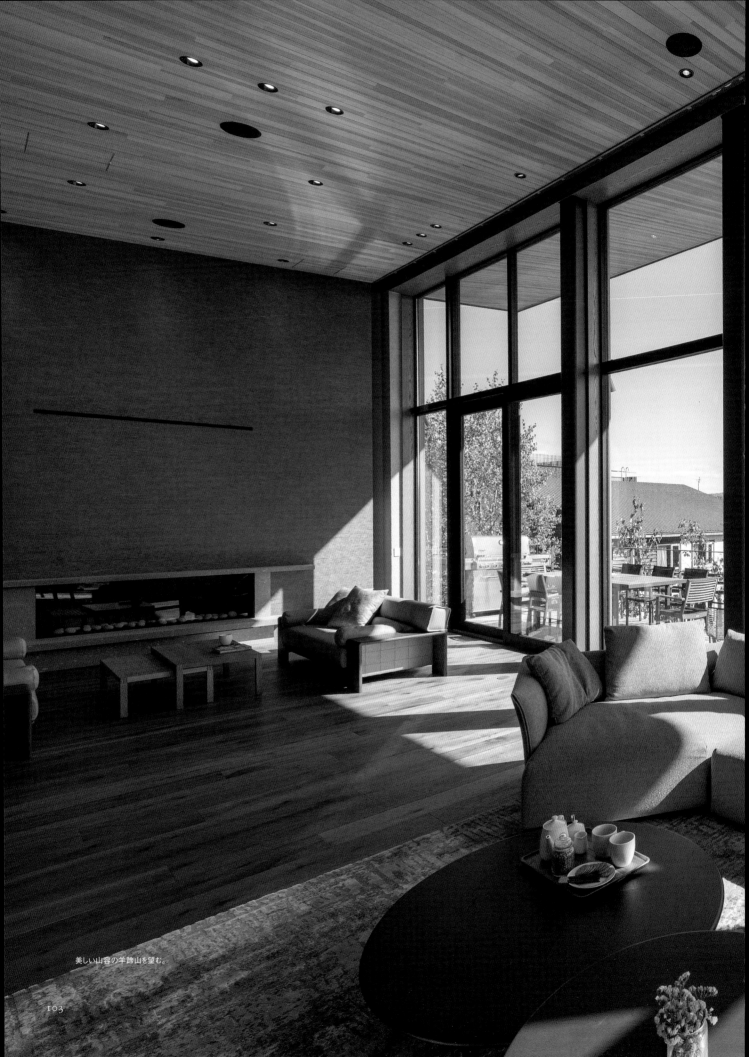

美しい山容の羊蹄山を望む。

天然素材を活かした家
A RESIDENCE THAT MAKES USE OF NATURAL MATERIALS

1.タモをふんだんに用いた3階のLDK。
2.外壁には杉羽目板と杉のルーバーを使用。

1

2

天然素材を活かした家
A RESIDENCE THAT MAKES USE OF NATURAL MATERIALS

Harmony with Nature

This rental vacation home looks out on Mt. Yotei, also known as "Ezo Fuji" (the Mt. Fuji of north Japan). The owner wanted a space featuring the warmth of wood, in a simple, monotone, modern design.

The starring role of the house design is played by the magnificent view of the Hokkaido landscape. The three-story steel-framed building was conceived to maximize the building coverage ratio and floor area-to-site area ratio. In the living-dining-kitchen (LDK) area on the third floor, overlooking Mt. Yotei, floor-to-ceiling glass offers both a wonderful view and sense of openness. The two living rooms are located adjacently to allow multiple simultaneous use.

Since the ski lodge-residence can accommodate up to 18 people, entertainment was a key concern. On the (ground-level) first floor is a genkan entrance hall, garage, and a drying room for ski boots, as well as an entertainment room for movies, reading, and games that adjoins a jacuzzi bath and sauna area.

On the second floor are four Western-style bedrooms and one in Japanese style, each with an en suite bathroom. To give the spaces a comfortable and relaxing feel, extensive use is made of natural wood, mostly tamo (Japanese ash).

The exterior walls are made of panels and louvers of sugi cedar, but to avoid a monotonous design without visually clashing with the surrounding natural environment, galvalume steel sheeting and natural stone are also employed. A spacious balcony adjoins the LDK space, making this ski lodge-residence an ideal place for people to immerse themselves in nature.

1

2

1.ジェットバスの横にはサウナを備える。
2.1階のバーコーナーとテレビも見られるジェットバス。

天然素材を活かした家
A RESIDENCE THAT MAKES USE OF NATURAL MATERIALS

自然に調和する落ちついた外観。

天然素材を活かした家
A RESIDENCE THAT MAKES USE OF NATURAL MATERIALS

最大10名が着席できるダイニング。

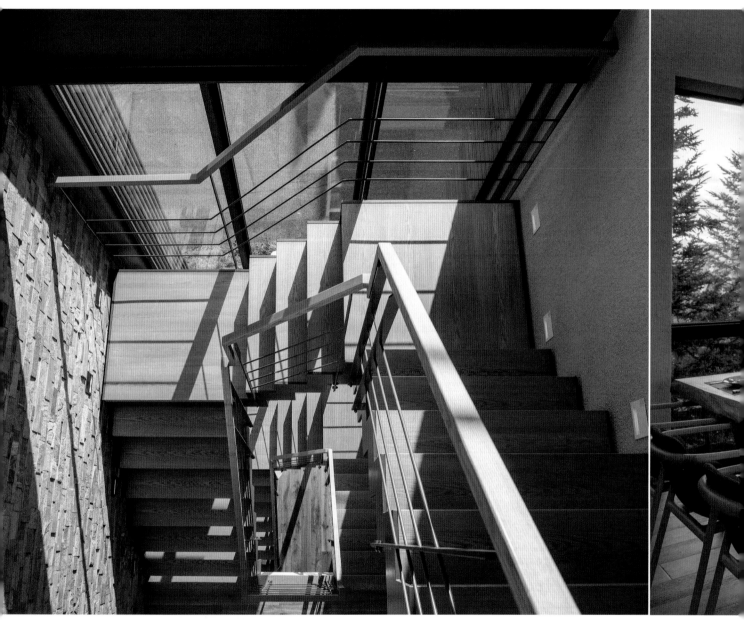

1

2

1. 3層を貫く階段。
2. 2階にある和室の寝室。幾何学的な障子がモダンな印象を与える。

天然素材を活かした家
A RESIDENCE THAT MAKES USE OF NATURAL MATERIALS

1.優雅なプライベート空間を演出するバスルーム。
2.洗面化粧台はホテルのようなたたずまいに。
3.木材を基調としたサウナルーム。

1
—
3　2

必要最低限の家具でシンプルにまとまった寝室。

天然素材を活かした家
A Residence that Makes Use of Natural Materials

1.テラスにはバーベキュー機器を備える。
2.3階の中心にダイニングがある。

自然との調和

蝦夷富士の別名をもつ羊蹄山を望む、1棟貸しのコンドミニアム。オーナーの希望は、モノトーンでシンプルなモダンデザインを基本としながら、木の温もりが感じられる空間だった。

主役はなんといっても、北海道の雄大な景色である。建ぺい率と容積率を最大限に使い、鉄骨造3階建ての建物を計画。LDKを3階に配置し、羊蹄山に面して床から天井までの全面開口にすることで、眺望と開放感を味わえる。連続して2つのリビングを設け、多様な使い方ができるようにした。

最大18名が宿泊できるコンドミニアムだからこそ、エンターテインメント性を追求した。1階は玄関、車庫、スキーブーツなどの乾燥室、映画や読書、ゲームを楽しむエンターテインメントルーム、そこに連続してジェットバスとサウナを用意した。

2階には洋室4部屋と和室1部屋の寝室、各寝室はバスルームを備えたエンスイートタイプで、タモを中心として天然木を多用することで、ゆったりとくつろげる空間とした。

外壁には杉羽目板や杉板のルーバーを用いて、周囲の自然環境になじむよう意図しつつ、ガルバリウム鋼板や自然石を組み合わせて単調なデザインにならないよう配慮。LDKには広々としたバルコニーを設け、大自然と一つになれるコンドミニアムとなっている。

Chapter 3 : Urban Residences for Living with Unlimited Richness in Limited Spaces

第 3 章　限られた空間に、無限の豊かさを生む都市邸宅

日常の喧騒を忘れさせる家
A RESIDENCE FOR FORGETTING THE CLAMOR OF DAILY LIFE

大庇の水平ラインが落ちつきを演出する。

118

都会で優雅なリゾート気分

光は時に人を穏やかにし、時に空間をドラマチックに彩る。
光のコントロールが空気感を決めると言っても過言ではない。
光と素材の調和が、リゾート地のような静穏な空気をつくり出す

An Elegant Resort Atmosphere

Light can have a calming effect, or it can enhance the drama of a space.
It's fair to say that the ambience of a space is determined by how the light is controlled.
A harmony of light and materials can create a serene atmosphere like a resort.

日常の喧騒を忘れさせる家
A RESIDENCE FOR FORGETTING THE CLAMOR OF DAILY LIFE

白やベージュを基調としたリビング。家具を差し色にした。

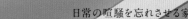

日常の喧騒を忘れさせる家
A Residence for Forgetting the Clamor of Daily Life

大庇が室内に入る光をコントロールする。

日常の喧騒を忘れさせる家
A RESIDENCE FOR FORGETTING THE CLAMOR OF DAILY LIFE

2 | 1

1.夜は温かな照明の光で満たされる。
2.パブリックスペースに置かれたエッチング加工を施したガラステーブル。

日常の喧騒を忘れさせる家
A Residence for Forgetting the Clamor of Daily Life

天井高まである大理石の壁が空間の伸びやかさを強調する。

隣家側は壁で囲み、段差を活かしてベンチをしつらえている。

Tranquil Air

A chalk-white mansion in a quiet residential district. On opening the door, one is greeted by an expansive space of profound serenity. A home that exudes refinement and elegance, balanced with a tangible warmth and peacefulness.
The husband-and-wife owners, who are attentive to every detail of their lifestyle, were seeking both privacy and a sense of openness. A courtyard-style plan was used to meet this requirement. All rooms are positioned to look out to the open two-story-high courtyard space, so that the courtyard can be directly experienced from every part of the house. The interior and the exterior are connected by the floor of beige tiles and divided by double doors with grid style bars, evoking the air of a stately European residence.

Eaves extend all the way around the courtyard. By limiting the natural light that enters the house, they give the illumination of the interior a gentle quality. Sunlight passing through a recess between the eaves and second floor generates dramatic, constantly-shifting shadows on the white walls. Outdoor furniture under the eaves serves as an in-between space for leisurely passing some time, without fear of getting wet by rain.
The living-dining-kitchen (LDK) area on the first floor is a single, flowing space. While the white and beige of the plaster and tiles are the underlying hues, bold-patterned marble on the wall gives the living room a strong focal point. The calmness of color scheme is juxtaposed by the iron grids of the doors. The gentle harmony of light and materials makes this residence feel like a place of healing.

日常の喧騒を忘れさせる家
A RESIDENCE FOR FORGETTING THE CLAMOR OF DAILY LIFE

1.アールの天井が印象的な2階の寝室。
2.大人数で食卓を囲めるダイニング。
3.2階にはファミリーダイニングを設けている。

静穏な空気

閑静な住宅街に建つ白亜の邸宅。扉を開くと、そこには静けさに満ちた空間が広がっている。洗練さとエレガンスさを漂わせながらも、人を温かく包み込む穏やかさも持ち合わせている。

暮らしの細部までこだわるオーナー夫妻が求めたのは、プライバシーの確保と開放感の両立だった。そこで中庭型のプランを採用。2層吹き抜けの中庭に面して各空間を配置し、どこからでも中庭を感じられるようにした。床はベージュのタイルで室内外を連続させ、観音扉には格子をあしらっており、まるでヨーロッパの邸宅を訪れたかのようである。

中庭を囲むように巡らせているのが大庇である。この庇で光をコントロールすることにより室内は穏やかな光となる。大庇と2階床の間にスリットを設け、そこから差し込む光が白い壁に刻一刻と変化するドラマチックな陰影を描き出す。庇の下はアウトドア家具を配し、雨に濡れることなく心地よく過ごせる中間領域として活躍する。

1階のLDKはひとつながりの伸びやかな空間である。漆喰やタイルなど白やベージュを基調としつつ、リビングの壁には大胆な石目の大理石をフォーカルポイントに。格子扉のアイアンが、穏やかなカラーコーディネートを引き締める役割を果たしている。光と素材の柔らかな調和による癒しの邸宅が完成した。

人を呼び寄せる家
A Residence that Draws People In

プライベートとパブリックの隙間

光は空間の印象をドラマチックに変えてくれる。
あえて光を絞って陰影を味わう一方で、明るさも享受する。
傾斜地という立地が、光が多彩に変化する邸宅をつくり出した。

Niches Between the Private and Public

Light can dramatically influence the impression of a space.
The light is consciously focused to bring out shadows, but also to enjoy the areas of brightness.
This residence, on a sloping site, harnesses the expressive power of lighting in a wide variety of ways.

彫刻のようなデザインの螺旋階段。

人を呼び寄せる家
A RESIDENCE THAT DRAWS PEOPLE IN

A RESIDENCE THAT DRAWS PEOPLE IN

リビングからは緑の借景を独り占めできる。

人を呼び寄せる家
A RESIDENCE THAT DRAWS PEOPLE IN

石とコンクリートによる洗練された外観。

天井や壁はチャコールグレーでムラをつけて塗装。

135

1.ダイニングキッチンは高低差をつけて場を分けた。
2.タモを染色した壁面が空間の印象を引き締める。

2
1

人を呼び寄せる家
A Residence that Draws People In

2階には吹き抜けに面してスタディースペースを設けた。

漆黒で仕上げたオーディオルーム。

Manipulating Light

To take advantage of the sloping site and maximize floor area, the residence was planned with four stories; two above and two below ground. The way light enters the building, the materials employed, and the colors used were all carefully studied to give each of the upper and lower levels their own very distinct ambience.

With its dark gray marble-toned tiles and undressed concrete, the lower level gives a sense of massiveness and solidity. The openings in the exterior are purposely narrowed down to concentrate incoming sunlight, so that light is guided from the upper to lower levels. The walls of the entrance and stairway hall on the second basement level (B2F) are rendered with a special plaster finish, resulting in a visually dramatic space featuring moire patterns created by the diffuse reflection of light from the areaway on the higher level.

In contrast, the upper floors are bright and refreshing spaces. The living room on the (ground-level) first floor features a high atrium-style ceiling with a curtain wall of double-layered glass and custom-made steel sashes, so as not to obstruct the view of the shakkei ("borrowed scenery") outside. The materials and colors were carefully coordinated to make the space light and bright and to avoid visual monotony. To soften reflection and create a sense of depth in the space, wall and ceiling surfaces are finished in a textured charcoal gray, while layers of real materials, such as the dark brown-stained tamo (Japanese ash) used for the wall storage and wooden beams on the atrium ceiling, give a sense of massiveness.

There is also study space and private room on the second floor and an audio room on the first basement floor (B1F). The mood of this residence changes with the scenes of daily life.

光を抑えた玄関ホール。壁の左官仕上げに光のモアレが描かれる。

人を呼び寄せる家
A RESIDENCE THAT DRAWS PEOPLE IN

光がたっぷりと入るリビング。

光を操る

　この邸宅は傾斜地を活かし、2層分を地下扱いとした4階建てにすることで床面積を確保。光の入り方や素材、色彩をコントロールし、上層部と下層部でまったく異なる世界観をつくっている。

　下層部はダークグレーの大理石調タイルとコンクリート打ちっ放しによって、マッシブなボリュームを感じられるよう計画した。あえて開口のボリュームを絞り込み、差し込む光の量を抑えることで、上層から下層へと光が導かれるようにしている。地下2階にある玄関と階段ホールの壁には、特殊な左官仕上げを施し、上階のドライエリアからの光が乱反射し、モアレを生み出す印象的な空間に仕上げている。

　一方、上層部は明るくさわやかな空間である。1階のリビングには吹き抜けを設け、2層分のガラス張りとし、借景を楽しむ眺めを妨げないよう特注のスチールサッシを採用。たっぷりと明るさを取り込み、空間が単調な印象とならないよう素材や色彩を細かに調整した。壁や天井は風合いのあるチャコールグレーにすることで光の反射率を抑え、空間に深みを感じられるイメージとし、ダークブラウンに着色したタモの壁面収納や吹き抜けの天井面に設けた木製の梁など、本物の素材を重ねることで重厚感をもたせた。

　2階にはスタディルームと個室、地下1階にはオーディオルームを配し、生活シーンに合わせた変化を演出する住まいとなった。

ヒトとモノの重厚感を高める家

A Residence that Heightens the Profundity of People and Things

落ちつきを取り戻す

都心部にありながら自然を感じられるコートハウスが完成した。
自然を切り取った中庭は小宇宙のような存在だ。
小さな自然にも、人はほっと心が癒され、安らぎを感じる。

Restoring Serenity

Even a small slice of nature soothes the heart and bestows peace of mind.

A courtyard, cut out of nature, is like a microcosm.

In this residence designed around a courtyard, one feels immersed in nature, in spite of the inner-city location.

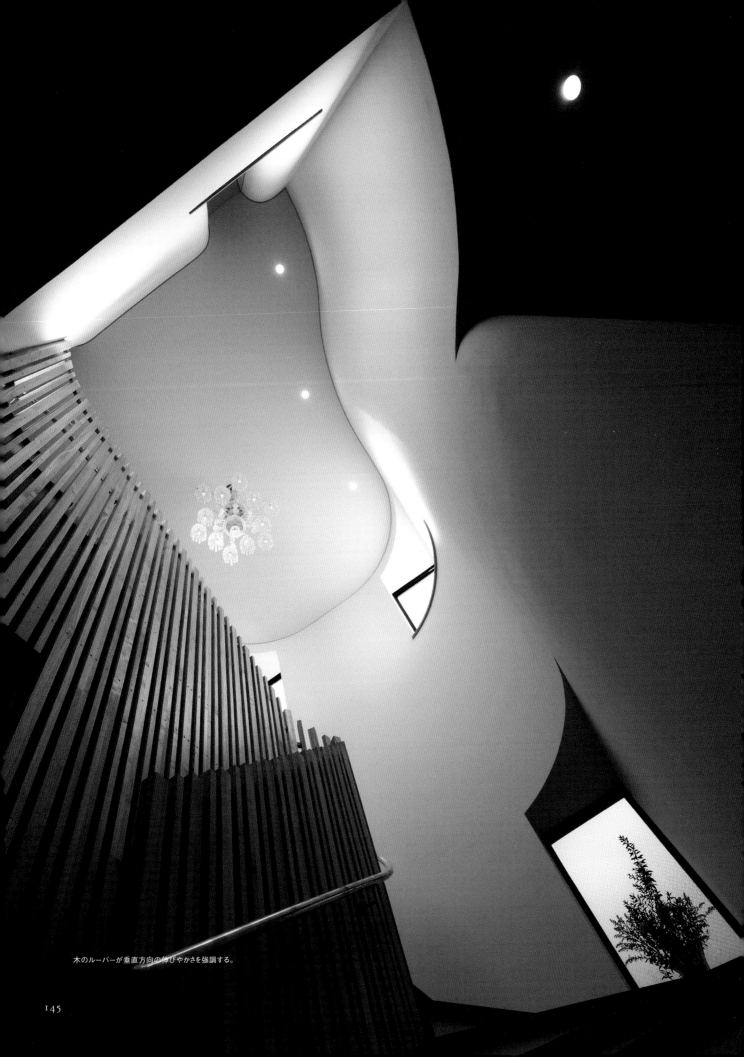

木のルーバーが垂直方向の伸びやかさを強調する。

ヒトとモノの重厚感を高める家
A RESIDENCE THAT HEIGHTENS THE PROFUNDITY OF PEOPLE AND THINGS

格子天井が水平方向の広がりを生み出す。

ヒトとモノの重厚感を高める家
A RESIDENCE THAT HEIGHTENS THE PROFUNDITY OF PEOPLE AND THINGS

中庭には石畳のテラスを設けた。

湾曲したタイル貼り外壁が街並みに溶け込む。

ヒトとモノの重厚感を高める家
A Residence that Heightens the Profundity of People and Things

中央の間仕切り壁が緩やかに場を分ける。

ヒトとモノの重厚感を高める家
A Residence that Heightens the Profundity of People and Things

2階に設けた和室。

A Courtyard is a Microcosm of Nature

Despite a very convenient city location, this home is in a residential district that retains an air of calm and elegance, with streetscapes replete with historical interest. The owner wanted to take full advantage of the location's charm, but also to secure a completely private space, by blocking the lines of sight from the nearby high-rise apartment buildings and expressway.

Since the site is long and narrow, the house is designed around a courtyard. Every room is positioned to face the courtyard, and a 7-meter-high retaining wall around the house ensures both openness and privacy.

Although there are dividing walls in the interior, doors are absent. All the spaces are connected openly to each other, to highlight the building's expansiveness. The living-dining room,

which serves as an entertainment space, features a large opening onto the courtyard and a lattice ceiling with straight lines to enhance the sense of depth. The floor and fittings are made of tamo ash, nara oak, and other natural timbers from Hokkaido. The design is distinctly modern, but this natural wood lends the space a feeling of warmth and serenity.

On the second floor there is a theater room where the owner can luxuriously enjoy his hobby of watching movies and concerts. Equipped with a bar counter, its graceful black interior design conjures a relaxing atmosphere. The gym area, topped with the latest training equipment, is configured to offer enjoyable views of the courtyard and surrounding area.

And views of the courtyard from various angles calm the mind. This high-quality residence is ideally finished for spending special moments.

外壁に樹木の影が映し出される。

ヒトとモノの重厚感を高める家
A RESIDENCE THAT HEIGHTENS THE PROFUNDITY OF PEOPLE AND THINGS

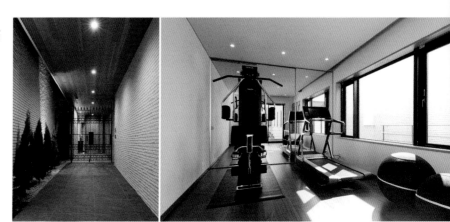

$$\frac{1}{3\quad 2}$$

1.漆黒の内装で仕上げたシアタールーム。
2.明るく、換気もしやすいトレーニングルーム。
3.細長い敷地を活かした長いアプローチ。

中庭という小宇宙

　利便性の高い都市部にありながら、歴史が培ってきた街並みを残す、落ちついた風情の住宅街。オーナーは、その立地の魅力を存分に活かしながら、隣接する高層マンションや高速道路からの視線を遮り、完全なプライベート空間を確保することを望んだ。

　奥に細長い敷地だったことから、中庭を配置したコートハウスのプランを採用。各居室を中庭に面して配置し、周囲には7mにも及ぶ高い擁壁を配置することで開放感とプライバシーの確保を両立した。

　室内は、間仕切り壁はあるものの、扉は設置せず、全体をひとつながりの空間とすることで広がりを強調している。中庭に面することで広がりを強調している。中庭に面せる上質な住まいに仕上がった。

して大きな開口を設け、ゲストをもてなすリビングダイニングには直線が奥行きを感じさせる格子天井を採用。床や建具にも北海道のタモやナラなどの天然木を多用。モダンなデザインを基調にしつつも、天然木が温もりと安らぎを感じさせてくれる空間となっている。

　2階には、オーナーの趣味である映画やコンサートの映像を楽しむシアタールームを設けた。バーカウンターをしつらえ、品格漂う黒い内装によって落ちつける居場所に仕上げている。最新のマシンをそろえたトレーニングルームは、中庭や周辺の眺望を楽しめるよう配置を工夫している。

　さまざまな角度からの中庭の眺めが、見る人の心を落ちつかせ、特別な時間を過ごせる上質な住まいに仕上がった。

静寂を楽しむ家
A RESIDENCE FOR BASKING IN STILLNESS

スペースの贅沢を享受する

無機質な素材が調和し、静寂を感じさせる邸宅。
グレーにまとめた空間にアートが浮かび上がり、美術館さながらのたたずまい。
光が壁にモアレを描き出し、建築そのものが芸術へと昇華する。

Enjoying the Luxury of Space

Inorganic materials harmonize to create a residence that confers serenity.
Art floats in a gray-colored space, evoking the air of a museum.
Lights generate moire patterns on the walls. Architecture is sublimated into art.

静寂を楽しむ家
A RESIDENCE FOR BASKING IN STILLNESS

Unified Beauty

This is a three-story house with an orderly facade in a residential zone. The owner's main requirements were to design a built-in garage and facade for three cars and a private space for the family to enjoy time together in a relaxed atmosphere.

His request has culminated in a house designed around a courtyard, featuring a three-story atrium. After passing through a long and narrow approach, one is welcomed at the end of the entrance way by a courtyard featuring olive tree, which stands as an iconic focal point with branches and leaves extended. The fact that the floors and walls are made of the same materials all the way from the approach to the courtyard helps to create a sense of spaciousness.

The living-dining-kitchen (LDK) space is on the second floor; the private rooms are on the third floor. The overall color scheme is rooted in gray tones, while the materials are predominantly inorganic; plaster walls, natural stone, floor tiles, and flooring. Thanks to the layout of the courtyard, the LDK space feels open and bright, rather than dark. And the owner's collection of contemporary art adds color. The gray hues of the space set off the artworks, resulting in a serene, museum-like atmosphere.

The staircase that extends from the first to third floor is visible through glass panels, further enhancing the sculptural presence. The walls are rendered with a special plaster finish that reflects light, creating dreamy moire patterns.

The wall of the kitchen, with its lowered ceiling, is colored in a much lighter hue to make it look spacious and to create a sense of cleanliness. All the fixtures and furniture items were also designed with obsessive attention to serve as works of art, resulting in a luxurious interior in which architecture and art are seamlessly harmonized.

階段室によって高さ方向の広がりが生まれている。

静寂を楽しむ家
A RESIDENCE FOR BASKING IN STILLNESS

1
―
2

1.下がり天井の間接照明がシャープなラインを強調する。
2.テラスは天然石調のタイル貼り。

個性的なペンダントライトがテーブルの上の世界をラグジュアリーに。

静寂を楽しむ家
A Residence for Basking in Stillness

天井もグレーに仕上げることで落ちついた雰囲気となる。

静寂を楽しむ家
A RESIDENCE FOR BASKING IN STILLNESS

1．玄関ホールから中庭を見る。
2．テラスにはルーバー越しに光が差し込む。

A RESIDENCE FOR BASKING IN STILLNESS

敷地の形状を活かした細長いアプローチ。

静寂を楽しむ家
A Residence for Basking in Stillness

3層分が吹き抜けた開放的な中庭。

統一した美しさ

住宅街に建つ、端正なファサードの3階建ての邸宅。オーナーが求めたのは、3台分の車を駐車できるビルトインガレージとファサードのデザイン、プライバシーを確保しながら家族がゆったりと団欒できる空間だった。

そこから導き出されたのが3層分を吹き抜けにしたコートハウスだった。細長いアプローチを抜けると、エントランスの奥ではシンボルツリーのオリーブが枝葉を伸ばす中庭が出迎えてくれる。アプローチから中庭まで床と壁を同じ素材でそろえたことで、広がりが生まれた。

2階にLDK、3階にはプライベートスペースがある。全体的にグレートーンを基調とし、壁の左官仕上げや天然石、床のタイルやフローリングなど無機質な素材感でまとめた。中庭の配置を工夫することで暗さを感じず、開放的で明るいLDKを実現。そこに彩りを添えるのが、オーナーが所有する現代アートの作品たちだ。グレートーンの空間にアートが映え、美術館のような落ちついた雰囲気を醸し出している。

ガラス越しに見える1階から3階までを貫く階段も、彫刻的な存在だ。壁には特殊な左官仕上げを施し、光が反射して幻想的なモアレが描かれる。

天井が下がったキッチンは広く見せるために壁の色彩のトーンを上げ、清潔感のある空間を意識。什器の一つひとつが美術品となるようデザインにこだわり、建築とアートが美しく調和した上質な空間となった。

美しき二つの融和

陶芸と建築の深遠

京焼の陶工、八代目清水六兵衞氏との出会いは16年前にさかのぼる。茶道の専門雑誌に声を掛けられ、対談する機会をいただいたのだ。

場所は京都・高台寺の「鬼瓦席」。灰屋紹益の好み、江戸時代前期の作で、簡素な木を適材適所で用いているところに共感を覚えた。清水氏も同様に空間の心地よさを感じていたようだった。それもそのはず。清水氏は大学で建築を学び、陶芸の道に進んでいるのだ。

私自身もこれまで多くの茶室を手掛けてきた。座ったときの窓の位置や、駆込天井の高さ、土や木、和紙といった自然素材の質感とその寸法……。細部にまで美意識が感じられる空間で、江戸期の京焼と茶室について心ゆくまで語り合ったのを、昨日のことのように覚えている。

もともと焼きものは好きではあったが、氏との対談以来、京焼について目がいく。野々村仁清の優美でふくよかなラインがある一方で、尾形乾山のような大胆さを持ち合わせる。

京焼とはいったいなんなのか――。

見れば見るほど、知れば知るほど、分から

なくなる。そのくらい奥が深い。

江戸時代初期、茶の湯の流行を背景に、東山山麓地域を中心に興隆した京焼。優れた陶工たちが登場し、初代清水六兵衞氏もその一人だった。

当代の八代目は歴代のどの作風とも異なる。なぜなら非常に建築的、構築的なのである。

製作した図面に合わせて正確に土の板を切り、統合させ、器体にスリットを入れて強度を操作する。構築的な一方で、土がもつ素材感、焼成の歪みなど、焼きものらしさを呈する。歳を経てますます磨きがかかり、空間と融和する作品を次々に発表している。

建築のなかで作品をどう美しく見せるか。あるいは、建築を美しく見せるために、どのような作品であるべきか――。その創作における思考を改めて語り合いたい。

陶芸と建築という違いはあれど、同じように日本の美を追い求めている者同士。16年という時間は、どのように美意識を深めてくれたのだろうか。

対談が叶い、今再び京都へ。静謐な空気が流れる高台寺の茶室「湖月庵」。まさに今回の舞台にふさわしい。

清水六兵衞

石出和博

なぜ大学で陶芸ではなく、建築を学んだのか

石出和博（以下、石出）　以前の対談は16年も前のことですが、清水先生はお変わりありませんね。

清水六兵衞（以下、清水）　石出さんも本当にお変わりなく。前回は高台寺の「鬼瓦席」でしたが、今

回は「湖月庵」で、こちらもすばらしい空間ですね。

石出　やはり清水さんは大学で建築を学ばれていたから、空間をよく見ていらっしゃいますね。まずお聞

きしたかったのですが、なぜ大学で建築に進まれたのか？　陶芸をするために建築を選んだのか、そう

でないのか。その理由が気になっていました。

清水　正直なところ、親に継ぐようにと言われたことはあまりなく、実のところ、学生の頃はまったく陶

芸のことは頭にありませんでした。六代目の祖父は日本画を学んでから陶芸の世界に入りました。私の

父である七代目は養子で、名古屋の生まれ。名古屋高等工業学校の建築科を卒業後、東京藝術大学

で鋳金を学んでから、陶芸の道に進みました。40歳を前にして「九兵衞」と名乗り、アルミニウムを主な素

材に用いて彫刻家として活躍したのです。そのような背景もあり、父は私が大学で建築を学ぶことについ

て反対することはなく、割と自由にさせてくれました。私は小さい頃から定規やコンパスで図面を描くの

が好きだったので、自然と建築の道を選んだような気がします。私は

大学時代に使っていたドラフターを今も使っています。もしも建築を学んでなかったら、今のような作品は

生まれなかったと思います。

石出　清水さんの作品は、非常に建築的だと感じておりました。先ほどドラフターを使うとおっしゃって

ましたが、形をつくる前に図面を描かれるのですか？

清水　まずは簡単にイラストを描き、そこから原寸の立面図を描いていきます。私にとっては図面で描い

たほうが細かな調整ができ、バランスも取りやすいのです。

石出　図面を作成してから立体にしていくのは建築も同じですね。図面どおりにつくっていくのですか？

それとも修正していくのですか？

清水　まず基本形は図面どおりにつくります。私の技法は「たたら成形」というのですが、最初はただの

立方体や直方体です。そこから一部を切り離し、切り取った部分に別のパーツを合わせていくのです。別の

パーツは図面で描いた後に型紙をつくり、板状に伸ばした粘土から型紙を使ってパーツを切り取ります。

石出　建築模型をつくるのと似ていますね。

清水　まさにそのとおりです。それを土に置き替えたような感じです。私の作品の場合は、側面を貼り

付けていくので、内部に支えのようなものが必要で、完成したら支えを取り除きます。建築を学んだから

こそのアプローチだと思っています。

京焼（清水焼）について
茶の湯の流行とともに発展した
400年以上続く焼きもの

江戸時代初期頃、茶の湯の流行を背景に茶碗や茶入などの茶陶の生産が盛んになり、京都の三条大橋の粟田口で瀬戸の陶工が登窯を築いたとの言い伝えが残る。1647年頃には野々村仁清が仁和寺の門前で御室焼を始め、この前後から洛北から洛東の寺院の領地を中心に、八坂焼、清水焼、御菩薩みぞろ焼、修学院焼、音羽焼、清閑寺焼などの窯が開かれた。清水焼は清水寺の参道界隈の五条坂でつくられていた焼きものを指し、土は清水寺が管理していた。仁清の弟子、尾形乾山（1663-1743）は1699年に鳴滝に登窯を築き、「古清水」と呼ばれる青・緑・金の三色の色絵陶器が完成。その後、初代清水六兵衞や欽古堂亀祐などの名工が次々に登場する。

清水焼は江戸時代から引き続き流行していた煎茶道具の生産により発展を続けた。明治には五条坂に京都市立陶磁器試験場を設立し、河井寛次郎をはじめ、東京や大阪の工業学校を卒業した技師たちが原料や釉薬などの最新の窯業技術を研究。現在の京焼の技術の基礎を確立した。窯ごとに異なる特色をもっといわれ、色絵や染付、天目など多種多様。現在は京都で焼かれている焼きもの全般を「京焼（清水焼）」と呼んでいる。

高台寺　湖月庵にて

京焼の多様さ、歴代で異なる作風

石出 先ほど歴代六兵衛ギャラリーを拝見させていただきましたが、京焼は非常にさまざまな釉薬の色やデザイン、技法があり驚きました。ほかの焼きものですと、土や技法がその産地の特徴になっていると思いますが、京焼はいかがですか？

清水 確かにほかの産地はそうかもしれません。京焼は「特徴がないことが特徴」とでもいいますか、さまざまな産地から原料をもってきて、京都で完成させていくつくり方なのです。なぜそのようなつくり方になったかというと、京都が産地だけじゃなく、消費地だからです。昔から公家やお寺などから注文を受けてつくってきた歴史があり、その結果多種多様な色やデザイン、技法が生まれたのです。

石出 なるほど。京都が最大の消費地だったと。

清水 さまざまなニーズに応えていくなかで幅が広がっていったのだと思います。それは陶芸だけに限らず、染色や織物、漆なども同じだったと思います。

石出 ギャラリーで初代から当代の清水さんまでずらりと並ぶ作品には圧倒されました。しかも、歴代で驚くほどに作風が異なりますね。作風をがらりと変えるのは勇気がいることではないですか？

清水 六兵衛窯は「先代と同じことをするな」という家風があり、作風を引き継ぎません。代々作風を継承していくことも非常にすばらしいことだとは思うのですが、先代より良いものをつくる、あるいはブラッシュアップしていくというのは苦労もあると思うのです。六兵衛窯は、がらっと作風を変えるので、何をつくろうか、というところから始まる。案外、気が楽かもしれません。創業から約250年間、常にその時代その時代の変化とニーズを察知してつくってきたので、自ずと新しいもの、時代の先端をいくものをつくれたのだと思います。また、初代から画家や文化人と交流があり、さまざまにコラボレーションもしてきたので、それも原動力の一つになっていると思います。一見ばらばらに見えますが、それぞれの作品からその時代の空気が感じられます。

石出 清水さんは大きな作品も多く手掛けられていますね。モジュールを一つひとつつくり、それをブロックのように組み立てていく作品は非常に建築的で、力強さを感じました。これらの作品の場合は、どのような場所に置かれることをイメージして制作しているのですか？

清水 大きな作品は、「パビリオンのようですね」とよく言われます。ギャラリーなどで展示される場合は、前もって天井高や床の素材などを確認しており、やはり場を意識してつくっていますね。大きな作品の際には、オパールラスター釉を使ったものもありますが、この釉薬は鏡面のように映り込むのです。人が近づくと人の影が映り込み、周囲の空間を反映する。人と作品、作品と空間の交流をイメージしてつくりました。

石出 何がきっかけでブロックのように組み立てていく方法を思いつかれたのですか？

清水 これはたたら成形の技法もありますが、吹き付けた釉薬が高温で溶け、エッジの部分の釉薬が動いて生地が表に出てくるからです。

石出 陶芸とは思えないほど、エッジのラインがはっきりと出ていますね。

六兵衛窯とは

1771年に初代清水六兵衛が京都・五条坂に開窯したことに始まる。初代は大阪の農家に生まれ、京都の五条坂にて海老屋清兵衛のもとで陶業を学んだ。海老屋から授けられた「きよ水」の印にちなんで「清水（きよみず）」の姓を名乗るようになる。初代は妙法院宮眞仁法親王の命により御庭焼で黒楽茶碗をつくり、「六目」の印を授けられた。これによって眞仁法親王の文化サロンに加わり、絵師の円山応挙や松村月溪（呉春）、文人の上田秋成、村瀬栲亭と親睦を深めた。

奔放で型破りな作風の二代、富岡鐵齋と共作した四代など、開窯以来250年余り、各代の当主が各々の特質を家伝の上に活かした作品を世に送り出してきた。各時代の画家や文化人との協業も特徴である。六代のときに会社組織として株式会社清六陶甸（現・株式会社キヨロク）を設立。現在は八代の監修のもとに、伝統的な京焼の作風を活かしつつ、食器から花器、インテリア、茶陶など現代のライフスタイルに合った製品を制作している。

対　　　　談

清水六兵衞
／
石　出　和　博

清水　現在は市内で登窯は使えませんから、電気窯に入るサイズのものしか焼けません。ギャラリーのインスタレーションの場合はある程度の大きさが必要なので、大きくする方法としてパーツを組み立てる方法にたどり着きました。

石出　それもやはり建築を学ばれていたからこそのアプローチですね。

清水　ブロックのように組み立てていくには精度が必要になります。現在の電気窯はコンピュータで温度を微調整できますが、以前は手動で温度のグラフをつけながら焼き、同じように温度を上げていくことで、ある程度精度をそろえることをしていました。技術の進歩があったからこそ、できた作品だともいえます。

陶芸の焼成からヒントを得た、カラマツの乾燥技術

石出　私は北海道のカラマツを建築に使うため、30年ほど前に乾燥技術を開発しました。それまでカラマツは曲がってしまうので建築材料には使えず、ほとんどがパルプになってしまっていました。それをどうしても100角の柱の形状のまま乾燥したくて、北海道の林産試験場に持ち込んだのです。最初は失敗ばかりで、バリバリに割れてしまいました。陶器も急に温度を上げたら割れてしまいますよね。

清水　そうですね。

石出　そのとき偶然、知り合いの備前焼の作家の方から、陶器を焼く窯の温度のグラフをいただいたのです。それでも割れるから、今度は100％の飽和蒸気の中で100度近くまで温度を上げ、徐々に温度を下げていく方法をとったら、うまくいくのです。蒸気を入れながら温度を上げていくのが鍵でした。

清水　蒸気があるのに乾くというのは、なんだか不思議ですね。土も分厚くて水分が多いと、焼いたときに破裂してしまいます。そこで、温度を200度弱で止め、いったん常温に戻し、それを何回か繰り返していくと中まで乾いていく。冷却のときに水分が抜けるらしいのですが、木の乾燥技術も同じだということですね。

石出　陶芸は土という天然の材料なので、木と共通点はあるのかもしれません。今では、その乾燥技術が全国で広まり、カラマツが活用されるようになりました。

清水　本日は陶芸と建築の共通点を見いだすことができ、非常に興味深いお話をお伺いすることができました。ぜひ今度は、作品で清水さんとコラボレーションをさせていただけるとうれしいです。

石出　それはうれしいお言葉です。こちらこそ、本日はどうもありがとうございました。

八代　清水六兵衛

七代の長男として1954（昭和29）年に京都に生まれる。襲名前の名前は柾博。1979（昭和54）年に早稲田大学理工学部建築学科卒業後、京都府立陶工高等職業訓練校で轆轤、京都市工業試験場で釉薬を学び、本格的に作陶活動に入る。1983（昭和58）年の朝日陶芸展'83でグランプリを受賞。その後も数多くの公募展において陶芸を重ね、1980年代から90年代にかけて陶芸表現が拡大する時代のなかで注目を集める。制作は図面にあわせて正確に土の板を切り、結合させる「たたら技法」。器体にスリットを入れることで強度を操作する、あるいは重力の力を利用するなど焼成による歪みへの力を意図的に造形化に取り入れている。2000（平成12）年に八代を襲名。以後、造形性をもった器物を中心に作品制作を展開する。2003（平成15）年に京都造形芸術大学教授となり、精力的な創作活動のかたわらで後進の指導にもあたっている。2005（平成17）年に2004年度日本陶磁協会賞を受賞するなど、現在の陶磁界を代表する一人である。

対　　談

清水六兵衞
／
石　出　和　博

Why did you study architecture instead of ceramics at university?

Kazuhiro Ishide: It's been 16 years since our conversation, but you don't appear to have aged at all, Kiyomizu-sensei.

Kiyomizu Rokubey: You haven't changed at all, either. Last time we talked at the Onigawara-seki teahouse here at Kodai-ji; this time we are at Kogetsuan, another wonderful space.

Ishide: Having studied architecture at university, you must have an acute sense of space. To begin, I wanted to ask you why you chose to study architecture at university? Did you choose architecture to help you develop as a ceramic artist? Or not? I was wondering about the reason.

Kiyomizu: Honestly, my father never really pressured me to take over from him. In fact, as a student, I never even thought about pottery. My grandfather, Rokubey VI, studied Japanese painting before entering the world of ceramics. My father, Rokubey VII, who was adopted into the family, was born in Nagoya. He only took up the path of ceramics after studying architecture at Nagoya Higher Technical School and then metal carving at Tokyo University of the Arts. He was even active as a sculptor, using aluminum as his main material, under his artistic name Kyubei took on before his 40s. Given his background, my father never opposed the idea of me studying architecture at university. He allowed me to do what I liked pretty much. Since I was a very young, I liked to draw with a ruler and compass, so choosing the path of architecture felt quite natural. I still work with the same drafting machine I used when I was at university. If I had never studied architecture, I don't think I would be producing the works I make today.

Ishide: Your works seem very architectural to me. You just mentioned that you use a drafting machine. Do you create drawings before shaping your works?

Kiyomizu: I start with a simple illustration, but I end up preparing full-scale elevation drawings. Drawings make it easier for me to make detailed adjustments to get the right balance.

Ishide: It's the same in architecture. You start with drawings and then translate the design into three dimensions. Do you follow your drawings exactly? Or do you modify them?

Kiyomizu: I start by making the basic shape according to the drawing. I use a technique called tatara forming. I begin with just a cube or a cuboid. Then I cut off a part of the clay and attach separate parts to it. To create the separate parts, I start with a drawing, then make a paper pattern of the part. Next, I use the pattern to cut out the part from a sheet of stretched clay.

Ishide: It's similar to how architectural models are made.

Kiyomizu: Exactly! Except that I am working in clay. To create my works, I attach the sides, which means that I need some kind of support inside the piece. When the piece is formed, I remove the support. This approach might also be the result of my architecture study.

The diversity of Kyo-ware, styles that change from one generation to the next

Ishide: I visited the Rokubey School gallery earlier. I was surprised by the variety of glaze colors, designs, and techniques used in Kyo ware ceramics. The clay and techniques used in other styles of ceramics are usually characteristic of the locality. What about Kyo ware?

Kiyomizu: This tends to be true for other production areas. You could say that the characteristic of Kyo ware is that it lacks a distinctive character. A wide variety of raw materials are brought in from different areas, to be worked and turned into finished products in Kyoto. This is explained by the fact that Kyoto is a major center of consumption, as well as production. In Kyoto there is a long history of making ceramics on commission for court nobles, temples, and the like. For this reason, a wide range of colors, designs, and techniques were developed here.

Ishide: I see! Kyoto was the biggest area of consumption.

Kiyomizu: Ceramic artists catered to such a diversity of needs

---

About Kyo ware (Kiyomizu-yaki)

A Living Ceramic Art Tradition That Emerged from the Popularity of the Tea Ceremony Over 400 Years Ago

Around the early Edo period (1603–1867), production of teacups, tea caddies, and other tea-related ceramics was flourishing, driven by the popularity of the tea ceremony. According to legend, a potter from Seto (Aich Prefecture) set up a climbing kiln at Awataguchi near the Sanjo Bridge in Kyoto.
In about 1647, Nonomura Ninsei started the Omuro Kiln in front of the main gate of Ninna-ji Temple. Starting at around this time, many other kilns, including Yasaka-yaki, Kiyomizu-yaki, Mizoro-yaki, Shugakuin-yaki, Otowa-yaki, and Seikanji-yaki were established in Kyoto, mostly in the vicinity of temples in the northern and eastern districts of the capital. The term "Kiyomizu-yaki" (Kiyomizu ware) refers to pottery produced in the Gojozaka, the area around the sloping approach to Kiyomizu-dera Temple, using clay controlled by the temple.
In 1699, Ogata Kenzan (1663–1743), a disciple of Ninsei, built a climbing kiln at Narutaki, where he created colored pottery in blue, green, and gold, in the style known as Ko-Kiyomizu (Old Kiyomizu). Later still, a succession of other master potters emerged, including Kiyomizu Rokubey I and Kinkodo Kamesuke.
The Kiyomizu-yaki tradition continued to grow and evolve through the production of sencha (green leaf tea) utensils, which had been in vogue since the Edo period.
In the Meiji period (1868–1912), the Kyoto Municipal Ceramics Testing Laboratory was established on Gojozaka. It was here that Kawai Kanjiro and other technicians who had graduated from technical schools in Tokyo and Osaka studied raw materials, glazes, and the latest ceramic techniques. Their work laid the foundations for the ceramic technology of today's Kyo ware.
There is also a wide variety of styles that characterize each kiln within the Kiyomizu-yaki school, such as iroe (colorful painted), sometsuke (blue on white), and tenmoku (black glaze). Today, all pottery produced in Kyoto is known as Kyo-yaki (Kyo ware), where the "Kyo" stands for "Kyoto." And, the name "Kyo-yaki" is synonymous with "Kiyomizu-yaki."

Rokubey Kiyomizu / **Kazuhiro Ishide**

Two Domains of Beauty Come Together

The Profundity of Ceramic Art and Architecture

My first encounter with Kiyomizu Rokubey VIII, a ceramic artist in the Kyo-ware tradition occurred 16 years ago. I was approached by a specialist tea ceremony magazine to engage in a dialogue with him.

The setting for our talk was the Onigawara-seki teahouse at Kyoto's Kodai-ji Temple. Built in the early Edo period on the aesthetic of Haiya Shoeki, a wealthy merchant with refined taste, its perfect use of simple wood made me feel very much at home. Kiyomizu-sensei seemed to feel equally comfortable in the space. Which should not be a surprise. Before taking up ceramics, he studied architecture at university.

In my time, I've worked on many tea rooms. I recall the position of the window while seated, the height of the sloping kakekomi ceiling, the texture of earth, wood, paper, and other natural materials and their dimensions... As if it were yesterday, I can remember how we talked to our heart's content about Kyo ware ceramics and teahouses of the Edo period, in a space that was aesthetically pleasing in every detail.

I have always loved pottery, but after my interview with Kiyomizu-sensei, I became strongly drawn to Kyo ware, in all its variety, from the graceful, full lines of Ninsei to the bold style of Ogata Kenzan.

So, what exactly is Kyo ware?

Well, the more you look into it and the more you know, the harder it is to answer this question. That's how deep it is.

In the early Edo period (1603–1867), when the tea ceremony was all the rage, Kyo ware ceramics flourished, most notably in the Higashiyama foothills of eastern Kyoto. One of the outstanding ceramic artists that emerged from this milieu was the founder of the Kiyomizu Rokubey school.

However, the style of Kiyomizu Rokubey VIII is quite distinct to that of any of his predecessors. It is a very architectural and structural style.

The master slices off sheets of clay and combines them precisely according to carefully prepared drawings. He also makes slits in the body of his pieces to manipulate strength. While his style is architectural, it also exhibits the typical characteristics of pottery, such as the texture of the clay material and the distortion of the firing process. As he gets older, Kiyomizu-sensei's work has become more refined. He has produced a succession of works that harmonize with the space they are installed in.

How does he make a work look beautiful inside the architecture? Or, to put it another way, what kind of works enhance the beauty of architecture? I would like to discuss the thinking behind the creative process again.

Notwithstanding their differences, ceramic art and architecture both involve the pursuit of a Japanese beauty. It's been 16 years since we last met, so I am curious to now how his aesthetic sense has deepened.

My desire to speak with Kiyomizu-sensei again has been fulfilled. So here we are, back in Kyoto. In the tranquil setting of the Kogetsuan teahouse at Kodai-ji Temple. A perfect setting for our conversation.

Institute. At first, we experienced nothing but failure. The wood would crack up into pieces. I imagine that the same thing happens with ceramics; if you raise the temperature too fast, it cracks, right?

Kiyomizu: Yes, correct!

Ishide: It just so happened that an artisan I knew who made Bizen ware ceramics gave me a graph of kiln temperature for firing pottery. I decided to apply it to drying the larch wood. But still the wood cracked. So, next, I tried to raise the temperature to nearly 100°C in 100% saturated steam, then slowly lower the temperature. This worked well! The key was to blow in steam while raising the temperature of the wood.

Kiyomizu: It's rather amazing that the wood dries despite the presence of steam. If clay is too thick and contains too much moisture, it bursts when it's fired. For this reason, we heat up the clay to a little under 200°C, return it to ambient temperature, then repeat this process several times until the inside of the clay is dry. Apparently, the water comes out during the cooling process, so the same thing probably happens with your wood drying method.

Ishide: Well, the ceramic is made of a natural material, clay, so there might be similarity with wood. Our drying method has spread throughout Japan, so larch wood is now used quite widely for building.

Today, we discovered some common features of ceramic art and architecture. It was a very interesting discussion. It would be great to collaborate with you on a work of art some time.

Kiyomizu: Thank you for your kind words. And thank you very much for the discussion today.

Kiyomizu Rokubey VIII

Born in Kyoto in 1954, as the eldest son of Kiyomizu Rokubey VII. His personal name was Masahiro. After graduating from Waseda University in 1979 with a degree in architecture, he learned to master the potter's wheel at the Kyoto Prefectural Advanced Vocational Training Center for Ceramicists, and studied glazes at the Kyoto Municipal Institute of Industrial Research, after which he set out in earnest to create ceramic art.
In 1983, he won the Grand Prize at the Asahi Ceramic Art Exhibition. He went on to receive numerous other awards at public exhibitions and his works attracted a great deal of attention throughout the 1980s and 1990s, a period when ceramic art expression expanded significantly.
He employs the tatara technique of precisely cutting clay slab and joining the cut pieces, based on prepared drawings. He also creates slits in his pieces to manipulate strength and intentionally incorporates distortion and drooping into his modeling by making use of the force of gravity and the heat of firing.
Since 2000, when he assumed the mantle of Kiyomizu Rokubey VII, he has principally produced figurative works. In 2003, he became a professor at Kyoto University of Art and Design, where on top of his energetic creative activities, he teaches younger aspiring artists.
In 2005, he received a 2004 Japan Ceramic Society Award. Today, he is a leading figure in the world of Japanese ceramics.

and demands that the range of ceramics they produced has naturally grown wider. This is true not only for ceramics, but also for dyeing, textiles, lacquer work, and other arts too.

Ishide: I was greatly impressed by the works on display in the gallery, all the way from the first generation of the school to your own works in this eighth generation. The styles of each generation were remarkably different. It must take a lot of courage to change styles so dramatically.

Kiyomizu: "Don't do the same thing as your predecessor" is virtually an unwritten rule of the Rokubey School; in other words, we don't carry on artistic styles across generations. It's a wonderful thing that a style is passed down from generation to generation, but if you can only focus on creating something better than the last generation, or on refining a particular style, it can be difficult. In our school, there is a complete change in style every generation, so we start out with an open mind artistically. "What shall I create?" Perhaps it might be more easier for us to make change. For 250 or so years since the school was established, I think we've naturally been able to create new, leading-edge products based on a sense of the changing needs and tastes of the time. Since the beginning, we've also engaged in exchanges and various kinds of collaborations with other visual artists and intellectuals. So, that is another driving force behind our work. Although at first glance all the works you saw may appear very diverse, they all convey an aspect of the time they were created.

Ishide: You've created many large works. The works that you compose by creating modules one by one and assembling them like blocks are very architectural and powerful. When you create such works, do you imagine the space that they will be installed in beforehand?

Kiyomizu: People often tell me that my large works look like pavilions. When I exhibit in a gallery, I check the ceiling height and flooring material in advance. So, yes, I'm very aware of the place where my work will be shown. For large works, I use an opal luster glaze, which gives the work a mirror-like finish.

When someone approaches it, their image is reflected in the glaze, along with the surrounding space. I've created works with the idea of expressing interchange, between the viewer and the work, and between viewer and the space.

Ishide: The edge lines are so clearly defined that it's hard to believe the works are ceramics.

Kiyomizu: This is due in part to the tatara shaping technique, but also because the sprayed glaze melts at a high temperature, causing the glaze at the edges to move and reveal unglazed material.

Ishide: How did you come up with your method of assembling blocks?

Kiyomizu: Currently, climbing kilns cannot be used in the city, so we can only fire pieces that are small enough to fit in an electric kiln. However, works for a gallery installation need to be of a certain size. To solve this problem, I hit on the idea of assembling multiple parts to make larger works.

Ishide: I guess this approach also came out of your architecture study.

Kiyomizu: It takes a lot of precision to assemble pieces like blocks. The latest electric kilns are computer-controlled, so you can really fine-tune the temperature precisely. So, I first fire manually and record a graph of the temperature. I can then program the kiln to raise the temperature in the same way, to get the necessary precision. It's fair to say that these works were made possible by technological advancement.

Larch drying technique inspired by ceramic firing

Ishide: About 30 years ago, I developed a drying technique to enable the use of Hokkaido larch wood for building construction. At that time, larch couldn't be used as a building material because it tended to bend. Most of it ended up as pulp. One way or another, I wanted to make use of it, so I took some of the wood along to the Hokkaido Forest Products Research

---

About the Rokubey School

It all began in 1771 when Kiyomizu Rokubey I opened a kiln in the Gojozaka district of Kyoto. Born into a farming family in today's Osaka prefecture, he studied pottery under Ebiya Seibei in Gojozaka, Kyoto. He took the family name "Kiyomizu" after the seal given to him by Ebiya. On the order of the Prince Masahito, the abbot of Myoho-in Temple, he made a set of black Raku-ware teacups at the imperial court, for which he was awarded the seal "Rokume." This allowed him to join the cultural salon of Prince Masahito, where he made friends with painters Maruyama Okyo and Matsumura Gekkei (Goshun), and the writers Ueda Akinari and Murase Kotei.

Over a period of more than 250 years since the kiln's founding, the heads of every generation of the school, such as the Kiyomizu Rokubey II, known for his uninhibited, trailblazing style, and Kiyomizu Rokubey IV, who collaborated artistically with (painter and calligrapher) Tomioka Tessai, produced works that imposed their individual characteristics on the family tradition. Throughout the generations, collaboration with painters and cultural figures has been a feature of the school.

During the reign of Kiyomizu Rokubey VI, the school established a company, Kiyoroku Toto Co., Ltd. (now Kiyoroku Co., Ltd.). Currently, under the direction of Kiyomizu Rokubey VIII, the company continues to utilize the traditional Kiyomizu-yaki style to produce a range of products to suit contemporary lifestyles, including tableware, flower containers, interior decorative pieces, and tea-related ceramics.

Chapter 4 : Residences of Materials that Embody Traditional Japanese Beauty

第4章　素材が日本の伝統美を体現する邸宅

視界を広げてくれる家
A RESIDENCE THAT EXPANDS VISION

溢れ出る自然の光

伝統的な日本家屋でしか醸し出せない空気がある。
一方で、現代的なモダン空間にも西洋の美しさが備わる。
それら2つを共生させることで 唯一無二の心地よさが生まれる。

Natural Light in Abundance

There is a certain feeling that only a traditional Japanese house can produce.
Yet, modern, contemporary spaces also offer a Western sense of beauty.
In coexistence, the two styles can give rise to a uniquely pleasing atmosphere.

銅板葺きの屋根は経年で落ちついた暗褐色へと変化していく。

視界を広げてくれる家
A Residence that Expands Vision

Contrast and Harmony

The owners of this residence, a couple who had lived abroad for a long time, yearned to live in a Japanese-style house. They wanted to live out the rest of their lives in a home that was modern and Western in style, yet also evocative of traditional Japanese materials and techniques. Thus, the design concept of the residence was wakon-yosai, or "Japanese spirit with Western learning," with a strong emphasis on the former element.

The residence includes both a main house (omoya) and a detached annex (hanare). The design of the main house is distinctly modern. A living-dining area of just over 50 m² features a coffered ceiling of a classic Japanese architectural design, showcasing the beauty of the house's timberwork. The natural wood floor and ceiling are finished in a dark color to lend a sense of mass and solidity, while light fixtures integrated into the ceiling lend the space a sense of largeness and openness, taking full advantage of the ceiling height.

The detached annex, on the other hand, is where the owners can fully enjoy the Japanese architectural charms. The positioning of stones, moss, and wood are calculated precisely to conjure an air of that ancient Zen ideal of "the serenity of a mountain retreat even amidst the bustle of the city." The design employs a copper-shingle roof, deep eaves, engawa veranda, and other traditional Japanese house features, including interior features such as yukimi shoji screens and a tokonoma alcove. Thanks to these elements, the house exudes a very Japanese aesthetic.

In contrast to the main house, with its Western design that takes in abundant natural light from outside, the annex design controls the incoming light to create shadows. Thus, these two buildings of contrasting yet harmonious styles manage to enhance each other's appeal.

1.離れの内部は駆込天井とした。
2.玄関アプローチから離れまでは露地をしつらえた。

1

2

視界を広げてくれる家
A RESIDENCE THAT EXPANDS VISION

格子天井がリビングの広がりを感じさせる。

2 | 1

1.ダイニングはテラスに面している。
2.本格的な和庭が母屋と離れをつなぐ。

視界を広げてくれる家
A Residence that Expands Vision

書斎は庭側に黒御影石の土間を設けた。

視界を広げてくれる家
A RESIDENCE THAT EXPANDS VISION

1
—
2

1.母屋のホールは濃い色に仕上げた天然木を使用。
2.グレーのタイルを用いたバスルーム。

192

母屋と離れのバランスを考え、壁に柔らかい印象の琉球石を使用。

視界を広げてくれる家
A RESIDENCE THAT EXPANDS VISION

曲線の屋根とバルコニーが特徴的な母屋のファサード。

対比と調和

海外生活が長く、日本家屋への強い憧れを抱いていたオーナー夫妻。洋式のモダンな空間のなかに、日本古来の素材や技術を感じさせる終の住処を思い描いていた。そこでこの邸宅では、和の精神性を主軸とした「和魂洋才」の考え方を取り入れ、設計を進めていった。

この邸宅には、母屋と離れがある。前面道路から続く長い階段アプローチを上がっていくと、徐々に和庭の先に離れの銅板葺きの屋根が垣間見える演出だ。

母屋はモダンデザインをベースとし、31畳という広さのリビングダイニングは天井を日本建築の「格子天井」とし、木組みの美しさを見せた。床と天井に用いた天然木は濃い色で仕上げて重厚感を醸しつつも、照明を格子天井内に組み込むことで、天井高を活かした開放感溢れる大空間をつくり上げた。

一方の離れは、日本建築そのものを楽しむ場所である。石と苔、木の配置を緻密に計算し、市中山居を感じさせた。銅板葺きの屋根をはじめ、深い庇や縁側など、伝統的な日本家屋の特徴を取り入れ、内部は雪見障子や床の間など日本の美意識を感じさせるしつらえとした。

外光をふんだんに取り入れる西洋的なデザインの母屋に対し、離れは光の入り方をコントロールして陰影をつくり、趣向の異なる建物の対比と調和が、互いの魅力を引き立て合っている。

和と洋が融合する家
A RESIDENCE THAT FUSES JAPANESE AND WESTERN STYLES

日本の伝統を
再解釈する

和の静謐さとは何か——。
それは光と影の関係であり、
内と外のつながりである。
そこには、日本らしい階調がある。
階調のなかに美を見いだし、
モダンな空間へと昇華させた。

石積みの曲線を描く壁が室内外をつなぐ。

Reinterpreting Japanese Tradition

What is this Japanese style of tranquility?
It is the interplay of light and shadow,
the connections between inside and outside.
Gradations that are uniquely Japanese.
The beauty in these gradations is discovered
and distilled to create a modern space.

和と洋が融合する家
A Residence that Fuses Japanese and Western Styles

ダイニングは2段高い場所にあり、目線が変わる。

1
2

1.高低差をつけることで空間を緩やかに分けている。
2.湾曲する壁が室内へと誘う。

和と洋が融合する家
A Residence that Fuses Japanese and Western Styles

間接照明によって浮いたようなアプローチのステップ。

A Residence that Fuses Japanese and Western Styles

玄関を入ると、ガラス越しに和室が出迎える。

Gradations of Light and Shadow

Stepping inside this residence, one is struck by an unmistakable hint of a Japanese ambience in a modern space.

Beyond the genkan entranceway, a Japanese-style room is glimpsed through glassed door panels. The graceful curve of the exterior wall seems to spontaneously usher visitors deeper into the house. This gently flowing line from outside to inside leads onward and deeper. It is as if the whole building were a spiral corridor.

Though it is not a purely Japanese residence, a distinctly Japanese tranquility can be felt in this seamless transition between outdoors and indoors. The wood panel ceilings and stonework walls continue outdoors, with deep eaves that serve the same function as those transition areas in traditional Japanese houses known as engawa, creating a pleasant veranda-like space. Curves and straight lines are skillfully combined, helping the character of each to stand out.

There is also a discernible Japanese spirit, reflected in the way light and shadow are captured. The modern living and dining areas are bathed in abundant light, with minimal shadows. In contrast, the illumination in other areas, such as the entryway, is subdued. By making extensive use of curves in the rooms and lengthening the lines of flow, the connection between spaces naturally becomes darker, and the expressions of light and shadow change every time one moves in the house. The contrast between brightness and darkness heightens the drama between them.

The subtle shifts in light and shadow that murmur to the senses signal the passing of time. This residence is a good example of a modern reinterpretation of classic Japanese architectural design elements.

和と洋が融合する家
A RESIDENCE THAT FUSES JAPANESE AND WESTERN STYLES

屋外の天井も曲線を描く。

和と洋が融合する家
A Residence that Fuses Japanese and Western Styles

1
―――
2

1.陶器の浴槽と檜の壁が和の趣を感じさせる。
2.浴室から眺めることができる坪庭。

光と影の階調

室内に足を踏み入れると、モダンな空間でありながら、そこはかとなく和の空気が漂う。

玄関の先にはガラス戸越しに和室が垣間見える。自然に奥へと誘われるのは、この邸宅の外壁が優美なカーブを描いているからだ。外から中へ緩やかな流れをつくり、その流れに沿って奥へと進んでいく。まるでこの建物全体が螺旋の回廊のようである。

この邸宅は純然たる日本家屋ではないが、和の静謐さを感じさせるのは、室内外が連続するように設計されているからである。板張りの天井と石積みの壁面が屋外まで続き、深い軒下は日本家屋の中間領域と同じ役割を果たし、縁側のように心地いい。曲線と直線をうまく組み合わせることで、お互いの個性を際立たせている。

さらに、光と影のとらえ方にも、和の精神性が反映されている。モダンなリビングダイニングは光をふんだんに取り入れ、影を少なくした一方、玄関などは照明を抑えている。室内にも曲線を多用し、動線を長く取ることで、空間と空間のつながりは自ずと暗くなり、移動するたびに光と影の表情も変化していく。明るさと暗さのコントラストがより互いを印象づけている。

五感にささやきかけるような光と影の繊細な変化は、時の移ろいにも似ている。日本家屋の要素をモダンに再解釈した好例だといえる。

和の心が生活に根差す家
A RESIDENCE ROOTED IN JAPANESE SPIRIT

Inviting Nostalgia

To the Japanese, living in a forest-rich country, trees evoke nostalgia.
Their presence is seen as a source of comfort and healing.
This tranquil residence is filled with the warmth of wood and light from a courtyard.

中庭の四方をガラス張りの回廊と居室が囲む。

208

郷愁を誘う

森林大国に住む日本人にとって、木は郷愁を誘い、
安らぎと癒しを与えてくれる存在である。
木の温もりと中庭の光に満たされた、穏やかな邸宅である。

和の心が生活に根差す家
A Residence Rooted in Japanese Spirit

縦格子が室内に繊細な光を導く。

和の心が生活に根差す家
A RESIDENCE ROOTED IN JAPANESE SPIRIT

中庭のガラス張りが空の景色を映し込む。

和の心が生活に根差す家
A Residence Rooted in Japanese Spirit

The Presence of a Courtyard

A courtyard adds richness to life. The brief for this residence called for a traditional Japanese aesthetic and abundant use of natural materials. It was also designed as a comfortable space in which a family can relax and feel at ease, with functional bedrooms and bathrooms. All of these requirements were fulfilled in the form of a house constructed around the four sides of a square courtyard terrace.

The use of wood gives the Japanese modern exterior a very warm look. Paneling of lauan (Philippine mahogany), stained in a tranquil dark brown tone, lends the residence a refined look.

After passing through a long approach, one arrives at an elegantly appointed entrance court. In the daytime, the water surface of the shallow pool wavers in the breeze, while at night, illuminated trees, planted as a focal point, warmly welcome visitors.

The courtyard terrace is enclosed on all four sides with glass surfaces, giving the interior a feeling of openness and brightness. Inside the glass, corridors run all the way around the courtyard, and the brightly lit courtyard comes into view from every room of the house. Achieving such openness in a timber structure is no easy task.

The living-dining area features a 3.5-meter-high atrium-style ceiling, with bold vertical latticework over the glass on the second floor. Light gently enters the room through the lattice.

Without any doors blocking the way in or out, the master bedroom on the second floor feels open. The bathroom, shower booth, washbasin area, and toilet are all integrated into the space in a hotel-like layout. Thus, the space is both relaxing and functional, with the soothing presence of the courtyard always at hand.

2

1

1.中庭はアウトドアリビングとして使われている。
2.中庭越しに家族の様子が感じられる。

2階の主寝室には広いバルコニーが隣接する。

和の心が生活に根差す家
A RESIDENCE ROOTED IN JAPANESE SPIRIT

$$\frac{1}{3 \quad 2}$$

1.リビングには暖炉を設置。
2.水盤のあるエントランスコート。
3.長いアプローチ。風合いのある土物のタイル石の壁にルーバーが影を落とす。

キッチンの上にはロフトがあり、2階の主寝室とバルコニーでつながる。

和の心が生活に根差す家
A RESIDENCE ROOTED IN JAPANESE SPIRIT

1
―
2

1.照明で演出したホテルライクな主寝室。
2.壁一面に梅の壁紙をアートのようにあしらった。

中庭の存在

　中庭は暮らしに豊かさを与えてくれる。

　この邸宅に求められたのは、和の風情と自然素材をふんだんに使うこと。そして家族が安心してくつろげる心地よい空間、機能的な寝室と水まわりだった。それらすべてを叶えたのが、中庭テラスを中心としたロの字型のプランだ。

　外観は、木の温もり溢れる和風モダンのたたずまい。ラワンの羽目板張りで上質なイメージを演出し、ダークブラウンの落ちついた色調で塗装した。

　長く延びるアプローチを抜けると、優雅なしつらえのエントランスコートが広がっている。昼間は水盤の水面が風に揺らぎ、夜はライトアップされるシンボルツリーが優しく出迎えてくれる。

　中庭テラスは四方をガラス張りとし、室内に開放感と明るさをもたらした。中庭を囲むように回廊を回し、どの居室からも明るい中庭が視界に入るよう計画している。これだけの開放感を木造で実現するのは簡単なことではない。

　リビングダイニングは天井高3・5mの吹き抜けとし、開口部には大胆な縦格子を採用。格子越しに入る穏やかな光が室内を満たす。

　2階の主寝室は遮るドアもない開放的なつくり。浴室やシャワーブース、洗面スペース、トイレを一体としたホテルライクなプランを採用している。くつろぎと機能性を両立した、常に中庭とともにある空間となった。

家は人の愛着で骨董品となる
Through Human Affection, Residences Become Charming Antiques

石出和博
Kazuhiro Ishide

古くならず深くなる

　1995年当時、建築材の約8割が安価な輸入材で占められていた。東南アジアの森は伐採されてハゲ山になり、大雨で土砂崩れが起きるといったニュースを見て、私は心が締め付けられた。

　日本は森林大国である。こんな近くに木があるのに、なぜ使わないのだろうか。日本で育った木は、日本の高温多湿の気候風土にも適しているはずである。

　家づくりでまず重要なのが素材だ。木や土、石といった本物の素材は時間とともに味わいを増し、古くならずに深くなる。

　私は北海道の木材を使って家を建てているが、子どもの頃にカラマツを植林するアルバイトをしたことがあった。カラマツは成長が早いうえに強度があり、炭鉱の坑木として使われ、戦前戦後に道内にたくさん植えられていた。

　しかし炭鉱が閉山し、人工林だけが残された。山は手入れされずに荒廃し、北海道で大きな社会問題となっていた。

　それらのカラマツは曲がる、割れるなどの理由から、ほとんどパルプにされていたのである。

　芦別には自分が植林したカラマツもあり、思い出もある。なんとか建築材として使えないだろうか——。

このカラマツを使いたい。そんな思いから北海道と林野庁を説得し、なんとか支援を受けることができた。

大学の研究者や林業の専門家とともに、木の乾燥技術と流通の仕組みを考えていった。4年間を費やして独自の乾燥加工技術を開発し、原木の確保から製材、流通、設計、建築までの新しい住宅供給システムを確立することができた。

木材は50年ほど経った間伐材を利用している。たとえ細い材であっても、加工して集成材にすれば構造材として十分使える。なるべく木は余すことなく使いたい。そして、家を建てた際に使った分の木を植樹するようにした。

また、林産試験場と共同で新しい建築金物を開発することで、耐久性の高い住宅が建てられるようになった。釘を使用していないので解体が容易で、数十年後の建て替え時にも、解体した構造材の約8割を再利用できる。これらは法隆寺や薬師寺などの木材を再利用する方法から学んだことである。

欧米では100年以上の建築も多く、古ければ古いほど価値があると考えられている。残念ながら、日本では古いと価値がなくなってしまう。私は100年以上もつ家を建てたいと思っている。そうすれば、森林の健全な成長と利用のバランスを守ることができる。

建築を志して

　建築を志したのは27歳だった。

　私は、戦後間もない北海道芦別の米農家に生まれた。減反政策のため18歳のときに廃農し、当時札幌に工場をつくったばかりのビール会社に入社することになった。仕事の後に夜学の建築短期大学に通い、必死で建築を学んだ。

　ずっと前から建築というものに憧れを抱いていた。初めて建築に触れたのは、小学校の修学旅行で訪れた京都と奈良。頭や心の柔らかい少年時代の私にとって、そこは憧れの世界となった。仏像や寺社の屋根が描く柔らかで優美な線、静謐なたたずまいに、なぜかふるさとに帰って来たようななつかしい気持ちになった。

　25歳のとき、会社の研究視察のために渡米したことが人生の転機となった。デンバーのある家庭にホームステイしながらビール会社の工場に通ったが、ホームステイ先のホストファーザーが偶然にも建築事務所の社長だった。彼は事務所にも法隆寺の五重塔の写真を飾っており、私にこう言った。

　今、ＳＤＧｓや国産材利用、ウッドショックなどが叫ばれているが、未来に豊かな住文化を守り引き継ぐには、持続可能な社会のあり方は当たり前のことだ。建築に携わる者は少なくとも50年後、60年後、あるいはもっと長いスパンでものを考えなくてはいけない。

「日本の古建築は本当にすばらしい。君は日本で建築を学んでいるのに、なぜその道に進まないのか。もったいない」と。

その言葉に帰国後の道は決まった。古来の建築の伝統を活かしながら、アメリカのような豊かな住環境を日本で実現したい——。

その夢を実現すべく、茶室建築を手掛けていた宮大工の会社に転職し、現場監督をしながら日本の伝統建築を学んだ。ノコギリの使い方から覚え、近い将来、必ず建築事務所をつくると心に誓った。

家づくりとは人生最大の遊び

日本には世界最古の木造建築である法隆寺がある。それなのになぜ、周囲の建物を見回しても、合理化と称した機能優先の工場製品ばかりが氾濫しているのだろうか。街並みは薄っぺらで、趣もなくなってしまった。戦後に効率ばかりを追求し、日本人は大事なことを忘れてしまってはいないだろうか。

建築は、お金を掛ければいいものができるわけではない。重要なのは、本物の素材を使うことである。木目を印刷したような新建材は、時間が経てばメッキのように剥がれ、みすぼらしくなってしまう。だから、20年、30年しか経っていないのに壊してしまうのだ。

戦後、日本人は車を買うように、家もシ

ステム化されたカタログから選び、「買うもの」と考えるようになった。家は商品ではない。家はつくるものだ。

動物たちは巣を繕う。繕うとは、自分の居場所を心地よいように整えていくことである。戦前は、父親たち自らが家を繕い、家と深く関わることが当然だった。欧米も家に対する思いが強く、竣工してからも暮らしに合わせてDIYでカスタマイズしていくなど、家は育てていくものだという文化がある。

家とは自らの人生観をかたちにしたものであり、美意識の集大成だ。家づくりは人生そのものであるにもかかわらず、現代の日本人は家や暮らしについて深く考えていない人が非常に多い。

「家づくりは人生最大の遊び」なのである。それを他人任せにするのは、あまりにももったいないのではないだろうか。

家に愛着があれば、どこか壊れたとしても修繕し、大事にしていこうと考えるだろう。愛着とは関わり方である。家づくりに深く関われば、自然と愛着は湧くものだ。

日本の美しさ

日本の美しさとは何か──。その問いに答えるのは非常に難しい。

若い頃は、暇にまかせては京都や奈良の茶室や数寄屋建築を見て歩き、茶道の稽

古にも通った。私は建築の材料やディテールが気になると、手で触れて確かめないと気がすまない質で、その積み重ねが審美眼を磨き、本物の建築をつくり出す基本になっていった。

戦後の日本人は、経済主義や合理化とともに、侘び寂びの感覚まで失ってしまったのではないだろうか。現代はプラスチックやビニールなどの新建材が暮らしのなかを包み、素材感をなくした無機質な空間が氾濫してしまっている。

あるカラーセラピーの研究家が現代の住空間にはゆらぎが足りないと言った。有機的な天然木の木目の流れ、土壁の風合い、障子越しにゆらぐ灯り……。和の意匠にはゆらぎがあり、五感を深く刺激する。

私は常々、侘び寂びを宿した本物の建築をつくりたいと思ってきた。そこに身を置くことで、現代人が忘れかけている、日本人特有の繊細な感覚や美意識を呼び覚ますと信じているからだ。

日本人の奥底に眠る感性を信じたい。日本には1400年以上前に建てられた法隆寺がある。それを見て、人は心を震わせるのだから。

建築を志してから半世紀近く、私は今もこの道を歩んでいる。

Kazuhiro Ishide

Through Human Affection, Residences Become Charming Antiques

Becoming Deeper and Richer, Not Older

In 1995, cheap imported timber accounted for around 80% of building materials. It was heart-wrenching to read that mountains in Southeast Asia were being stripped bare of trees, leading to landslides after heavy rain.

Japan is a forest-rich country. So, why can't we make use of all these trees we have such ready access to? Trees grown in Japan should be well suited to the hot and humid climate here.

The most important resource for building a house is materials. Over time, genuine materials like wood, earth, and stone develop a unique charm. They get deeper and richer with the passing of the years, not older.

I now build houses using timber produced in Hokkaido. As a child here, I had a part-time job planting karamatsu (Japanese larch) trees. Larch is both fast-growing and strong. Since it was used in the pits of coal mines, it was planted in large quantities in Hokkaido before and after World War II.

However, when the coal mines closed, only man-made forests remained. Mountain forests fell into disrepair, creating a serious challenge for Hokkaido.

Most of those larch trees ended up as pulp, because they were bent and split.

I remember planting some larch trees in Ashibetsu. I wonder if I could use them as building materials in some way.

I want to make use of this larch somehow. With this idea in mind, I managed to persuade the Hokkaido government and the Ministry of Agriculture, Forestry, and Fisheries to support me.

Together with university researchers and forestry experts, my team figured out a wood-drying technique and distribution mechanism. It took us four years to develop our own drying and processing technology, but this enabled us to establish a new housing supply system, spanning everything from securing raw timber to sawing, distribution, design, and construction.

For the lumber, we use trees cut for forest thinning, which are about 50 years old. Even thin wood can be used as structural timber if it is processed into laminated timber products. Our goal is to use as much of the wood as possible. We also planted trees to replace the ones we harvested for building houses.

The development of new fittings and mountings for construction, in collaboration with the Forest Products Research Institute of Hokkaido, has enabled us to build highly durable houses. Since no nails are used, disassembly is easy. This means that about 80% of the structural materials disassembled when it comes time to rebuild after several decades can be reused. This is something we learned from how wood has traditionally been reused at Horyu-ji, Yakushi-ji, and other temples.

Many buildings in Europe and the U.S.A. are over 100 years old. And typically, the older a building, the more valuable it is considered. Unfortunately, in Japan, the older the house, the lower its value. I want to build houses that will last for at least a century. If we do this, we can maintain a balance between the healthy growth and utilization of forests.

Today, we hear a lot of talk about the U.N.'s sustainable development goals (SDGs), using domestic timber, and "wood price shocks." I believe that if we just preserved and passed down a rich housing culture to future generations, we could achieve a sustainable society quite naturally. Everyone involved in architecture and construction needs to think 50 to 60 years ahead, or even longer.

The Aspiration to Build Houses

I was 27 years old when I decided to pursue a career in architecture and building.

I was born into a rice farming family in Ashibetsu, Hokkaido, shortly after World War II ended. Due to a policy of rice acreage-reduction, we abandoned farming when I was 18, so I joined a beer company that had recently opened a factory in Sapporo. After work, I attended night school to learn building construction at a junior college. I was very desperate to learn about building.

For a long time, I felt a strong aspiration to build houses. My first contact with architecture was during an elementary school excursion to Kyoto and Nara. For me, as a young boy with a fresh and flexible mind, these places were my dreamworlds. The soft, delicate lines and peaceful look of Buddhist statues and the roofs of temples and shrines stirred a powerful sense of nostalgia in me, as if I had returned to my hometown.

A major turning point in my life came when I traveled to the U.S.A. for a company study tour. I was 25 at the time. While visiting a brewery, I stayed with a family in Denver. The head of the household happened to be the president of an architectural firm. In his office, he had a picture of the five-story pagoda of Horyu-ji Temple. He told me that the ancient architecture of Japan was truly amazing. "Since you are studying architecture in Japan, wouldn't it be a pity not to follow that path?" he said to me.

It was these words that set me on the path I would take after I returned to Japan.

My goal was to utilize old Japanese architectural traditions to create rich living environments in Japan, like those enjoyed in the U.S.A.

To fulfill this dream, I switched jobs, to go and work for a company of temple carpenters that built Zen teahouses. While employed as a site supervisor, I learned all about traditional Japanese architecture. I learned how to use a saw and I vowed that one day soon I would set up my own architectural office.

Building a House is the Greatest Fun in Life

Japan is home to the world's oldest wooden structure, Horyu-ji Temple. Why, then, when we look at the buildings around us, do we see only a flood of mass-produced products that prioritize functionality in the name of efficiency? Our cityscapes have become flimsy and charmless. The single-minded pursuit of efficiency following World War II made Japanese people forget some important things.

It is not possible to build a good house by merely spending a lot of money. The key factor is to use genuine materials. New building materials with printed wood grain patterns tend to peel off like tinplate over time, resulting in a shabby look. That is why houses in Japan are often demolished after just 20 or 30 years.

Following the war, Japanese people started to think of a house as just another product; to be purchased from a catalog, just like a car. But a house is not a commodity. It is something that needs to be created.

Animals repair their nests. They care for their dwelling place to make it comfortable for themselves. Before the war, it was natural for people to mend their homes and become deeply involved with them.

Europeans and Americans tend to feel strongly about their homes. There is an established culture of nurturing homes and home environments. For example, after building a house, many people continue to improve and tailor their home to their specific needs by doing DIY work.

A house is also seen as an expression of one's outlook and aesthetic sensibility. Despite the fact that building a house is an essential part of life itself, too many Japanese people today give little thought to their homes or lifestyles.

There is no greater fun in life than building a house for yourself. So, it's a pity to leave it to others.

If we feel affection for the home we live in, we will always be willing to repair and care for it whenever it is damaged in some way. This sense of attachment and affection fosters involvement and engagement. Naturally, when you get deeply involved in building your house, you will also be committed to caring for it.

Japanese Beauty

What is Japanese beauty? This is a very difficult question to answer.

When I was young, I spent a lot of my spare time in Kyoto and Nara walking around to study the architecture of teahouse and sukiya-style buildings. I even practiced the tea ceremony. Whenever I was interested in a material or the detail of an architectural structure, I felt compelled to touch it to confirm it with my own hands. All these experiences allowed me to hone my aesthetic sense and build a foundation for creating genuine architecture.

With all the emphasis on economic growth and rationalization after the war, the Japanese people lost their sense of wabi-sabi (simplicity and beautiful imperfection). In our daily lives, we are increasingly surrounded by plastic, vinyl, and other synthetic building materials. And everywhere there are inorganic spaces that lack any feeling for materials.

A color therapy researcher has noted that modern living spaces lack organic variation and fluctuation.

Organic patterns of natural wood grain, the textures of earthen walls, and the glimmering lights seen through shoji screens... Traditional Japanese design is characterized by this kind of natural variation that deeply stimulates the physical senses.

I have always wanted to create genuine architectural constructions that embrace wabi-sabi. I believe that when I place myself in an environment, I tap into a delicate sensibility and aesthetic awareness that is uniquely Japanese. Sadly, I think that most people today have almost completely lost these things.

But I still have faith in this sensibility that lies deep within the people of Japan. After all, Horyu-ji Temple, constructed more than 1,400 years ago, is still with us. When people view it, their spirit is stirred and renewed.

Today, almost a half-century after setting out on my architectural career, I am still walking the path.

Profile

石出 和博
HOPグループホールディングス株式会社 代表取締役
ハウジングオペレーションアーキテクツ株式会社 代表取締役会長

1967年 北海道産業短期大学建築学部卒・北海道アサヒビール株式会社入社。
1973年 北海道中堅青年海外派遣事業で渡米、米国の建築に刺激を受け日本の伝統建築を学ぼうと帰国。
1974年 株式会社藤田工務店入社、宮大工の技術を学ぶ。
1989年 一級建築士事務所アトリエアム株式会社設立、伝統住宅、茶室などの作品を発表。
1997年 林野庁と北海道の支援を受け、国産木材を活用した新しい産地直送の住宅供給システム、HOPハウジングオペレーションアーキテクツ株式会社を設立、現在に至る。

主な受賞
1997年 グッドデザイン北海道
2000年 札幌商工会議所北の企業家奨励賞
2001年 林野庁長官賞
2006年 経済産業大臣賞
2010年 経済産業省環境特別賞

著書
フォトエッセイ集こころ紀行（須田製版）、ハウスドクター診察室（リプラン社）、石出和博とアトリエアムの世界（ART BOX社）、美しい日本の邸宅（幻冬舎メディアコンサルティング）など。

Kazuhiro Ishide
Representative Director & CEO of HOP Group Holdings Inc.
Chairman & Representative Director of Housing Operation Architects Inc.

1967 Graduates from Faculty of Architecture, Hokkaido Sangyo Junior College and joins Hokkaido Asahi Breweries, Ltd.
1973 Travels to the U.S.A. under a Hokkaido overseas youth dispatch program, becomes inspired by American architecture,
 and returns to Japan determined to study traditional Japanese architecture.
1974 Joins Fujita Koumuten Co., Ltd. and learns the specials skills of a temple and shrine carpenter.
1989 Launches ATELIER AM, a first-class architectural studio and starts creating traditional Japanese homes, tea ceremony rooms, etc.
1997 With the assistance of the Forestry Agency and Hokkaido Government, he establishes "Housing Operation" (HOP),
 a new housing supply system for utilizing domestic timber directly from the place of production, remaining its leader until today.

Major Awards
1997 Good Design Hokkaido Award
2000 Sapporo Chamber of Commerce - Northern Entrepreneur Encouragement Prize
2001 Forestry Agency Director-General Award
2006 Minister of Economy, Trade and Industry Award
2010 Special Environment Prize at "Japan Venture Awards 2010" hosted by Ministry of Economy, Trade and Industry of Japan

Books
"KOKOROKIKO (Mind book of travel note)" (photo essay collection) (Suda Seihan); "House doctor consulting room" (Replan Web Magazine);
"The World of Kazuhiro Ishida and Atelier AM" (ART BOX); "Japanese Beautiful Residence" (Gentosha), and more

関 恵里子
ハウジングオペレーションアーキテクツ株式会社 代表取締役社長

1992年 北星短期大学卒、輸入インテリア会社・法律事務所を経て
2002年 HOPアーキテクツ入社・社長室配属
2003年 HOP東日本立上げに従事。インテリア統括
2006年 HOPグループ広報統括部長就任、新時代のweb営業戦略を確立する。
2011年 HOP東日本統括部長就任・支社長兼務、全国展開への基盤を築く。
2013年 取締役就任
2015年 取締役東日本支社長・総務統括部長兼務
2016年 代表取締役社長就任、現在に至る。

Eriko Seki
President & Representative Director, Housing Operation Architects Inc.

1992 After graduating from Hokusei Gakuen University Junior College, worked for an interior importing company and law firm.
2002 Joins HOP and assigned to the president's office.
2003 Engages in the establishment of the Eastern Japan branch office, and supervises interior work.
2006 Appointed General Manager for PR of the HOP Group and works to formulate web marketing strategies in the new era.
2011 Appointed General Manager of HOP Eastern Japan branch office, as well as the branch office manager. Built infrastructures towards nationwide developments.
2013 Appointed a Director of HOP.
2015 Serves concurrently as a Director, President of HOP Eastern Japan branch office, and General Manager for General Affairs.
2016 Appointed President & Representative Director of HOP (current position).

Office			
	HOP札幌	札幌市中央区北4条西21丁目2番1号	TEL 011-615-7777
	HOP東日本	横浜市西区みなとみらい2-3-1クイーンズタワーA棟7F	TEL 045-224-8511
	HOP名古屋	名古屋市中区錦二丁目4番15号ORE錦二丁目ビル10F	TEL 052-232-0125
	HOP大阪	大阪市中央区今橋3丁目2番14号KPOビル6F	TEL 06-6484-5188

HOPグループ			
	一級建築士事務所アトリエアム株式会社 AM東京	横浜市西区みなとみらい2-3-1クイーンズタワーA棟7F	TEL 045-224-8522
	一級建築士事務所アトリエアム株式会社 AM大阪	大阪市中央区今橋3丁目2番14号KPOビル6F	TEL 06-6484-5188
	一級建築士事務所アトリエアム株式会社 AM札幌	札幌市中央区北4条西21丁目2番1号	TEL 011-621-8718

HOPデザインを支える建築家達
Chief Designers
supporting HOP Design

ハウジングオペレーションアーキテクツ株式会社（HOP）

北東　丈嗣　ハウジングオペレーションアーキテクツ株式会社 取締役設計統括部長
1997年　大阪大学工学部環境工学科卒
1997年　積水ハウス株式会社入社
2002年　株式会社コンプレックス入社
2004年　ハウジングオペレーションアーキテクツ設計部入社
2020年　取締役設計統括部長就任

Takeshi Hokuto　　Director & General Manager for Design, Housing Operation Architects Inc.

1997 BSc in Environmental Engineering, School of Engineering, Osaka University
1997 Joins Sekisui House, Ltd.
2002 Joins Complex Co., Ltd.
2004 Joins Design Department of HOP
2020 Appointed Director & General Manager for Design of HOP

原田　昌樹　ハウジングオペレーションアーキテクツ株式会社 取締役デザインセンター長
1996年　広島大学工学部建築科卒
1996年　原広司＋アトリエ・ファイ建築研究所入社
2007年　ハウジングオペレーションアーキテクツ設計部入社
2014年　取締役デザインセンター長就任

Masaki Harada　　Director & the Head of Design Center, Housing Operation Architects Inc.

1996 BSc in Architecture, Faculty of Engineering, Hiroshima University
1996 Joins Hiroshi Hara + Atelier Phi
2007 Joins Design Department of HOP
2014 Appointed Director & the Head of Design Center of HOP

渡瀬　猛雄　ハウジングオペレーションアーキテクツ株式会社 設計部長
1991年　北海学園大学工学部建築学科卒
1991年　ミサワホーム北海道株式会社入社
2005年　ハウジングオペレーションアーキテクツ設計部入社
2012年　設計部長就任

Takeo Watase　　The Head of Design Department, Housing Operation Architects Inc.

1991 BSc in Architecture and Building Engineering, Hokkai-Gakuen University
1991 Joins Misawa Homes Hokkaido Co., Ltd.
2005 Joins Design Department of HOP
2012 Appointed the Head of Design Department of HOP

斎藤　力　ハウジングオペレーションアーキテクツ株式会社 設計部統括マネージャー
2005年　東京造形大学造形学部デザイン学科環境計画専攻卒
2005年　MOMO株式会社入社
2013年　ハウジングオペレーションアーキテクツ設計部入社
2021年　設計部統括マネージャー就任

Tsutomu Saito　　General Manager of Design Department, Housing Operation Architects Inc.

2001 BA in Modeling Design, Tokyo Zokei University
2005 Joins MOMO Co., Ltd.
2013 Joins Design Department of HOP
2021 Appointed General Manager of Design Department of HOP

田村　昭人　ハウジングオペレーションアーキテクツ株式会社 設計部チーフマネージャー
2005年　室蘭工業大学大学院建設システム工学専攻修士課程修了
2005年　株式会社KEN一級建築士事務所入社
2012年　株式会社北デザイン建築工房入社
2014年　ハウジングオペレーションアーキテクツ設計部入社
2022年　設計部チーフマネージャー就任

Akihito Tamura　　Chief Manager for Design, Housing Operation Architects Inc.

2005 MSc in Architecture and Building Engineering, Muroran Institute of Technology
2005 Joins KEN-Architects Co., Ltd.
2012 Joins Kita Design Co., Ltd.
2014 Joins Design Department of HOP
2022 Appointed Chief Manager for Design of HOP

○ 撮 影

第 1 章

p012 - 027 　木田 勝久

p028 - 043 　木田 勝久

p044 - 059 　木田 勝久

第 2 章

p062 - 073 　木田 勝久

p074 - 085 　木田 勝久

p086 - 099 　木田 勝久

p100 - 115 　グレン・クレイドン

第 3 章

p118 - 129 　木田 勝久

p130 - 143 　渡辺 琢哉

p144 - 155 　木田 勝久

p156 - 167 　トニー谷内

p168 - 179 　田島 雄一

第 4 章

p182 - 195 　木田 勝久

p196 - 207 　木田 勝久

p208 - 221 　トニー谷内

○ プリンティング ディレクション

松本 年正 　HOPグループ 株式会社ラッププロジェクトオフィス　代表取締役

○ デザイン・装丁

松崎 理 　yd co.,ltd.

美しい日本の邸宅 2

二〇二三年三月二四日　第一刷発行

著　者　　石出和博

発行人　　久保田貴幸

発行元　　株式会社 幻冬舎メディアコンサルティング
　　　　　〒一五一〇〇五一　東京都渋谷区千駄ヶ谷四─九─七
　　　　　電話　〇三─五四一一─六四四〇（編集）

発売元　　株式会社 幻冬舎
　　　　　〒一五一─〇〇五一　東京都渋谷区千駄ヶ谷四─九─七
　　　　　電話　〇三─五四一一─六二二二（営業）

印刷・製本　瞬報社写真印刷株式会社

検印廃止
©KAZUHIRO ISHIDE, GENTOSHA MEDIA CONSULTING 2023
Printed in Japan ISBN978-4-344-94165-6 C2052
幻冬舎メディアコンサルティングHP　https://www.gentosha-mc.com/

本書についての
ご意見・ご感想はコチラ